Building Confidence:

Your Guide to Get Motivated, Be Assertive, Conquer Fear, and Empower Your Life for Success

Barrie Davenport

ISBN: 0692295844
ISBN-13: 9780692295847

Disclaimer

No part of this publication may be reproduced or transmitted in any form or by any means, mechanical or electronic, including photocopying or recording, or by any information storage and retrieval system, or transmitted by email without permission in writing from the publisher.

While all attempts have been made to verify the information provided in this publication, neither the author nor the publisher assumes any responsibility for errors, omissions, or contrary interpretations of the subject matter herein.

This book is for entertainment purposes only. The views expressed are those of the author alone, and should not be taken as expert instruction or commands. The reader is responsible for his or her own actions.

Adherence to all applicable laws and regulations, including international, federal, state, and local governing professional licensing, business practices, advertising, and all other aspects of doing business in the US, Canada, or any other jurisdiction is the sole responsibility of the purchaser or reader.

Neither the author nor the publisher assumes any responsibility or liability whatsoever on the behalf of the purchaser or reader of these materials.

Any perceived slight of any individual or organization is purely unintentional.

Your Free Gift

As a way of saying thanks for your purchase, I hope you'll enjoy "110 Empowering Essentials for a Confident Life" to help you determine where you can make positive changes for improvement and growth. Being a confident person involves all aspects of your life—from your relationships to your career. The key is to identify what you want to change in each area and create a plan of action to kickstart a real positive shift.

In "110 Empowering Essentials for a Confident Life," I offer dozens of suggested actions in each life area to inspire you toward action. Becoming a more confident person doesn't happen by itself. You can boost your confidence by recognizing the behavior of confident people, and then putting those into action in your own life.

Download this free report by going to
http://simpleselfconfidence.com/FREE

Contents

Introduction

If we all did the things we are capable of doing,
we would literally astound ourselves.

~Thomas Edison

YOU ARE CAPABLE of great things. You are capable of success and achievement beyond your wildest imaginings.

You have enough intelligence and plenty of available resources to create a satisfying, rewarding, and happy life for yourself. Perhaps you don't feel that way right now, but assume for a moment it's true. Everything you need, you already possess.

The only thing missing is the key to unlock all of that potential. Without the key, you remain incapacitated, unable to take action, speak up, make decisions, or take calculated risks.

In order to access your potential, you need a healthy amount of confidence—a firm belief in yourself and your abilities and the initiative to take action. Without confidence, regardless of how smart and talented you might be, you will remain stuck. You won't become the person you are meant to be.

Fortunately, the key to confidence is available to everyone— and that includes you. Although some people are predisposed to confident personalities, anyone can learn the skills of confidence and apply them daily. You can profoundly improve your feelings of self-assurance, ambition, sociability, and initiative.

The purpose of this book is to provide you the key to unlock your own self-confidence. I'll present practical, research-based information and exercises to improve your confidence, as well as challenge you to use your growing confidence to change your life.

I'm offering you a blueprint to rebuild yourself, using confidence as the bricks and mortar. A house built with bricks and mortar can withstand challenges, obstacles, and setbacks. These challenges are part of life for the confident and insecure alike.

When I was in my early twenties and applying for my first job out of college, I was sitting in my soon-to-be boss's office as she reviewed my resume. She excused herself for a moment, leaving my resume on her desk.

I peered over to see what she had written on it, hoping to see something like, "Amazing candidate. Brilliant. This is the one!" Instead she had written two words: "Blonde. Timid."

Over thirty years later, I still remember the sinking feeling I had walking out of that interview. I'd been reduced to two not so very positive words—certainly not the words I wanted to describe me. They sure didn't seem like hiring words.

Of course I *was* blonde and timid. I was a brand new college graduate with a major in English literature. I had little work experience, few marketable skills, and a degree with no clear career path.

When I got home, I shared the experience with my mom, and she encouraged me to get on the phone and let this woman know how much I wanted the job. "The squeaky wheel gets the grease," she reminded. I was filled with fear and self-doubt, but I made the call. I mustered up enough courage to sound eager and enthusiastic, even though I was feeling far from it. I got the job.

The memory of that event has stayed with me over the years. Although my confidence has grown as I've gotten older, there are still plenty of times when I'm not on my game and don't feel secure in myself. When this happens, I remember how taking just one small confident action, in spite of being fearful and insecure, opened the door to a twenty plus year career in public relations. It profoundly changed my life.

Small acts of confidence can create big opportunities. It all begins with the belief that confidence is possible. It can be improved, and you *can* change your life.

With this book, you'll learn more about confidence, what holds you back from it, and how you can start taking small, manageable actions to rebuild your confidence—even before you begin feeling confident.

I encourage you to begin this book knowing that confidence awaits you. You can and will feel good about who you are, secure in your abilities, eager to take action, and strong enough to remain confident in the face of challenges or setbacks. A confident, new you is waiting.

Who Am I?

My name is Barrie Davenport, and I run two top-ranked personal development sites, Live Bold and Bloom (www.liveboldandbloom.com) and Barrie Davenport (www.BarrieDavenport.com). I'm a certified personal coach, former public relations professional, author, and creator of several online courses on self-confidence, life passion, and habit creation.

My work as a coach, blogger, and author is focused on offering people practical strategies for living happier, more successful, more passionate lives. I utilize time-tested, research driven, action-oriented principles to create real and measurable results.

As a coach, I've learned through countless sessions with courageous, motivated clients that each individual has the answers within them. Every person has the wisdom and intuition to know what is best for themselves. Sometimes we simply need someone or something to coax it out of us and hold our feet to the fire so we follow through.

That's what I hope this book will do for you—coax out the self-awareness and confidence you already possess and motivate you toward positive action. There are some brief action steps at the end of each chapter. If you want to get the most from this book, take the time to complete the exercises immediately after you read the chapter, while the information is still fresh.

You now have the building blocks for confidence. The key to your potential is in your hand. It's up to you to unlock the door.

Barrie Davenport

Chapter 1:
Confidence and the Traits of Confident People

ACCORDING TO DICTIONARY.COM, self-confidence is "a realistic confidence in one's own judgment, ability, and power." Confidence is "full trust; belief in the powers, trustworthiness, or reliability of a person or thing"—in this case, you. Having self-confidence means you feel comfortable with, even happy with your ability to successfully navigate through life and move past life's problems or your own failures with the belief you are still capable and worthy.

In fact the foundation of confidence is the feeling of assurance in who you are and the ability to love and accept yourself, flaws and all. You view yourself from a perspective of optimistic realism and self-respect which is the result of living authentically, within your integrity and around your values. A confident person knows who they are, how they want to live, and can quickly move past failures and mistakes after an appropriate period of grief and self-examination.

You don't have to be a high achiever, financially successful, stunningly attractive, or super intelligent to have self-confidence. In fact, you can be a regular Jane or Joe and still have buckets of confidence. Although some people are born with a genetic predisposition to a positive attitude or a beautiful appearance, DNA certainly isn't everything. Confidence can be learned and nurtured, and there are specific skills that foster confidence. With these skills, you have the power to create your life rather than react to it. You have control over your destiny, and the only thing standing in your way is your belief about yourself—and perhaps a lack of knowledge about how to change your thoughts and beliefs.

Confidence also involves knowing yourself really well. You have examined your life and have a certainty about what's important to you, how you want to live, and who you want to be. An examined life offers a framework for confidence because it affords you security and boundaries. When you're flailing in life, uncertain of how to behave or what actions to take, you live in fear and confusion. Without direction or guiding principles, it is hard to feel self-confident.

Confidence doesn't require you to be always on top of your game, always assertive and in-control, always polished and sophisticated. It doesn't require fearlessness in every situation, nor does it mean you must be an extrovert or a public speaker. At its core, real confidence is about embracing your true self and learning to love that self while continuing to improve upon it. It's about defining your own personal operating system, based on your core values and integrity, and then designing your life around this system.

Please know if you are not self-confident now, you can be—if you are willing to make some changes. It will involve self-reflection, shifts in thinking, and changes in behavior. It will definitely involve practice and patience—but anything good does. Improving your confidence requires a healthy amount of self-esteem—enough positive feeling about your essential worth that you're able to like yourself and value your inner wisdom and judgment.

Many people confuse self-esteem and self-confidence, believing they are simply different names for the same concept. They are not the same, although they are closely related and interdependent. As mentioned earlier, confidence is faith in one's own abilities and judgments. In essence, it means you believe strongly you're capable, self-reliant, and resilient. Self-esteem reflects a person's overall appraisal of his or her own worth. Your self-esteem is based on your beliefs about your own inherent value as a person and your emotional view of those beliefs. You can certainly lack confidence and still have self-esteem. It's much more difficult to lack self-esteem and still feel confident about yourself and your abilities.

Below is a list of ten traits you generally see in confident people. As you read these traits, think about whether or not you possess them. This will be a good barometer of where you need to focus your self-confidence work.

1. Confident people are self-assured.

They believe in themselves and know their life fulfills a special purpose in the world. They know their strengths and have accepted their weakness.

Do you believe in yourself?

Do you have a life purpose?

Do you acknowledge your strengths and accept your flaws?

2. Confident people are ambitious.

They know what they want and easily define their goals and strive to achieve them.

Do you have a vision and goals for your life?

Are you actively working toward achieving them?

Can you act on them in spite of your fears?

3. Confident people are sociable.

They're skilled at navigating various social situations with ease. They are comfortable because they believe they belong in any environment. They can endear themselves to others and know how to take compliments and criticisms gracefully.

Do you feel comfortable in social situations?

Can you meet new people and talk with them easily?

Do you feel you belong just as much as the next person?

4. Confident people are healthily competitive.

They love to test their abilities against the best efforts of others, and they believe they can win, even when they've lost in the past. They know testing themselves makes them stronger.

Do you look to others to inspire and motivate you to do better?

Can you genuinely admire another person's ability even if you aren't there yet?

Can you see the value of challenging yourself even if you might fail?

5. Confident people are risk takers.

They take calculated risks because they like to stretch themselves, and they aren't afraid to lose or to be wrong. While they are confident in their abilities, they accept that nobody wins them all, and that likely they'll succeed the next time.

Are you willing to take reasonable risks in order to learn or improve?

Can you accept the possibility of failure without feeling devastated?

Can you see the value of failure for growth and learning?

6. Confident people are hard-working.

They know the best path to achieving their goals is through hard effort, no matter how exhaustive or arduous. They recognize success isn't always easy.

Do you have the emotional energy to put toward working hard?

Do you feel that your efforts will have a good outcome?

Do you feel enthusiastic or energize by tackling a project or problem?

7. Confident people are determined.

They never give up on their goals, even when it seems difficult or impossible. They know that it is better to try and fail and then try again, rather than to give up altogether.

Do you believe that you may need attempt a goal many times before you succeed?

Do you allow obstacles or problems to deter you from your goal?

Do you have the energy and faith in your abilities to test different avenues and options?

8. Confident people are accepting.

They take others as they come, no matter their flaws or shortcomings. Confident people recognize their own shortcomings and realize that the path forward is not about keeping other people down, but through lifting them up and accepting them.

Can you easily accept people as they are, even those close to you?

Do you try to find the faults in others to make yourself feel better?

Do you need to associate only with those who make you look better?

9. Confident people are shrewd.

Often awareness and cleverness breed confidence. Confident people are often good at quickly sizing up other people and figuring out social hierarchies and complicated situations.

Are you able to assess situations and people easily to see your best fit?

Do you feel "in touch" with the emotions and needs of those around you?

Can you respond easily and graciously to the needs of others?

10. Confident people are positive.

They know how to assuage doubts, overcome fears, and how to find the good even in bad situations. They understand failure is a part of everyday life, and that fresh starts are always possible.

> Do you feel happy and positive more often that sad or upset?

> Do you have the mental and emotional tools to quickly overcome negative thinking?

> Do you regularly feel gratitude for all of the good things in your life?

As you understand the traits of self-confidence, you can begin practicing some of these traits in your daily life, even when you may not feel confident at all. Through practice, you'll begin to rewire your brain so that self-confident actions feel more natural, giving power to the feelings of confidence as you began to act "as if" you possessed these traits.

Action Steps

After reviewing the traits of confident people, where do you see yourself possessing confidence? Where are you lacking in confidence? Answer the questions under each trait, and

make note of the traits you need to improve most.
Sometimes improving one trait will help improve the others.

Barrie Davenport

Chapter 2:
What Does DNA Have to Do with It?

THINK ABOUT THE closest members of your blood family—your parents, siblings, grandparents, and aunts and uncles. How is their self-confidence and overall outlook on life? Do they have similar personality traits to you or to each other?

There's no doubt DNA plays some role in our levels of confidence. Behavioral geneticist Corina Greven of King's College in London and her colleague, Robert Plomin of the Institute of Psychiatry, believe genetics determine the personality traits of confident people. Their research, published in the June, 2009 issue of *Psychological Science,* analyzes the hereditary component of confidence and its relationship to IQ and performance. By comparing 3700 pairs of genetically identical twins to non-identical siblings, they were able to determine the relative contributions of genes and the environment. They found that children's self-confidence is heavily influenced by heredity—at least as much as IQ is.

If you've inherited low confidence or introverted personality traits, it might feel you're destined to a life of insecurity and lackluster performance. Maureen Healy, children's health expert and author of the book *Growing Happy Kids: How to Foster Inner Confidence, Success and Happiness,* strongly believes otherwise. In a 2011 *Psychology Today* article, Healy suggests:

> Being a guide to so many parents and children on the topic of self-confidence, I can tell you that it is solely a skill to be mastered. There is no 'magic pill' that you take, and boom—you wake up feeling confident from the inside out. But there are certain ways to think, feel and be in the world that nudge you forward and help you develop the skill (hear me: I said skill) to believe in yourself wholly and completely.

She believes even if you are genetically wired with a less-than-sanguine personality, you can still improve your confidence when you learn some specific confidence-boosting skills. According to Healy, there are a host of behaviors and mindsets— from exercise to self-awareness—that if learned and adopted, can increase your natural sense of confidence.

The field of social and emotional learning (SEL), made popular in Daniel Goleman's 1995 book *Emotional Intelligence*, also supports the opinion that confidence isn't just shaped by one's DNA. Goleman's research shows that emotional intelligence (EQ) is the best predictor of a child's future achievement; better than any other single factor.

Says Goleman, "IQ is only a minor predictor of success in life, while emotional and social skills are far better predictors of success and well-being than academic intelligence." Of course achievement and success hinge on confidence—one of the cornerstones of emotional intelligence.

By learning the skills of emotional intelligence, many of which are outlined in this book, you have an enormous advantage in your personal and professional future. Dr. Maurice Elias, a leading child psychologist, researcher and expert on SEL from Rutgers University, suggests in his book *Emotionally Intelligent Parenting*, that emotional intelligence is "dramatically and positively predictive not only of academic achievement, but also of satisfactory and productive experiences in the world of work and marriage, even of better physical health."

Personality type, another inherited trait, also impacts one's future success in life. Researchers have found a correlation between extroversion and both self-esteem and happiness. People who are extroverts tend to report higher levels of both of these than do introverts. However, we must remember that extroversion is considered more socially acceptable in Western culture. Our society rewards extroverted behavior such as sociability, optimism, enthusiasm, and gregariousness.

So where does that leave the introverts? If you happen to live in Central Europe, Japan, or places where Buddhism, Sufism, and other inward focused religions are prevalent, you'll find that introversion is respected. For those of us introverts who live in Western Cultures, here are some important things to remember:

- According to Carl Jung, introverts more easily acknowledge their psychological needs and problems, whereas extroverts tend to be oblivious to them because they focus more on the outer world.

- Researchers have found that introverts tend to be more successful in academic environments, which extroverts may find boring.

- Introverts have more blood flow in the frontal lobes of their brains and the frontal thalamus, which are areas dealing with internal processing, such as planning and problem solving.

- Introverts make up 20 percent of the general population, but they comprise 60 percent of the gifted population.

- Although an introvert may enjoy less time with large groups of people, he or she enjoys interactions with close friends.

Although people with low confidence and low self-esteem might be introverts, introverts don't necessarily have low self-esteem. There are many outlets for introverts to experience confidence—through academic, intellectual, emotional, and relational pursuits and successes. Also, it's important to note that people fluctuate in their behavior all the time, and even extreme introverts and extroverts do not always act according to their type. Since personality type varies along a continuum, people can have a combination of both orientations. A person who is introverted in one situation may be extroverted in another.

Learning to act against type is healthy, and it's quite possible to learn to act against type in specific situations in order to improve confidence. For example, an introvert might not be comfortable making a speech to a large crowd, but she can master public speaking in order to feel confident about doing it when necessary.

Whether you're an introvert or an extrovert, it's important that you understand who you are and why you feel and behave the way you do. Understanding yourself will help you embrace your uniqueness rather than resisting it or feeling you should be someone you're not. Although it's true some people are born with a predisposition toward confidence and an optimistic outlook, those of us who didn't inherit these success genes aren't doomed to a life of self-doubt and failure. Any small improvement in confidence has the potential to affect major life change, just as one phone call did after my disastrous first-job interview.

In fact, those without the heredity component, who truly want to improve their confidence, may likely work harder to learn the skills of confidence than their genetically blessed counterparts. Even those with natural confidence and optimism must work to maintain it. It doesn't really matter whether nature or nurture shaped your confidence. Everyone must learn the emotional, social, and coping skills necessary to operate successfully in our complex and often challenging lives. Simply begin with who and where you are, and move forward with the skills you are learning.

Action Steps

Think about your close family members and their temperaments. Are they confident and extraverted? Do you have a genetic predisposition to being self-confident? Or do you follow a line of introverts who may be lacking in self-assurance?

If you want to know more about your personality and whether you are more introverted or extraverted, take this Free Online Personality test at http://www.humanmetrics.com/cgi-win/JTypes2.asp.

Chapter 3:
Your Brain on Confidence

HERE'S SOME GOOD news about confidence: if you alter your brain, boosting your self-confidence is a cinch. This doesn't mean you need brain surgery or mind-altering drugs. It does require you repeat small behaviors frequently enough so your brain carves out new neural pathways. There's an entire field of science that recognizes and studies the brain's remarkable ability to mutate and grow. It's a revolutionary, exciting science called neuroplasticity.

Neuroplasticity means our thoughts can change the structure and function of our brains. The idea was first introduced by William James in 1890, but it was soundly rejected by scientists who uniformly believed the brain is rigidly mapped out, with certain parts of the brain controlling certain functions. If a part of the brain is dead or damaged, the function is altered or lost. It appears William James knew what he was talking about. Scientists have since proven the brain is endlessly adaptable and dynamic. It has the power to change its own structure, even for those with the severe neurological afflictions. People with problems like strokes, cerebral palsy, and mental illness can train other areas of their brains through repetitive mental and physical activities.

Neuroplasticity is "one of the most extraordinary discoveries of the twentieth century," according to psychiatrist Norman Doidge, M.D., author of *The Brain That Changes Itself.* Neuroscience demonstrates the brain is constantly forming new neural pathways, removing old ones, and altering the strength of existing connections. This means the brain is able to adjust and adapt physically at any age to compensate for an injury or illness and to adapt to new behaviors, situations or changes in the environment. The brain is not fixed, but rather, it's like clay—a malleable structure that molds itself in response to information and experience.

One of the most significant findings has been the discovery that our brain doesn't stop growing when our body does; it has the ability to adapt and change right up to the end of our life. Just because we have well-established ways of processing information and responding to our environment, we're still capable of developing new and more constructive ways in the future. So what does this have to do with you and your confidence? It means by practicing repetitive confident behaviors, you can rewire your brain to create new neural pathways to cement real *feelings* of confidence. Every time you repeat a confident behavior, you're giving your brain a cue to recognize this behavior as automatic and real. Your brain will adapt to your behavior, and your feelings of confidence will follow suit.

If you add positive thinking and visualization to the repetitive behaviors, you're super-charging your brain's response to change. Jeffrey Schwarz, author of *The Mind and the Brain: Neuroplasticity and the Power of Mental Force,* made an extraordinary discovery while using the therapy he developed for his patients with obsessive-compulsive disorder. By actively focusing their attention away from negative behaviors and toward more positive ones, Schwartz's patients were using their minds to reshape their brains. They were effecting significant and lasting changes in their own neural pathways, using thoughts to change the structure of their brains.

World class athletes use visualization regularly to enhance performance and optimize the possibilities for success. But these techniques don't have to be limited to the psychologist's office, science lab, or the world of sports. They can be used by all of us in our efforts to change our thoughts and behaviors and ultimately create more satisfying lives.

Imagine this: every time you take a confident action or visualize yourself confidently succeeding, your brain is being rewired. New connections are forming and old ones are losing their potency. With your brain's remarkable ability to change, every day and every moment you have the capacity to reinvent yourself. By consciously choosing your actions and reinforcing them with repetition, positive thinking, and visualization, you have the power to act and envision yourself to a confident new you.

Here are some actions you can take in your daily life to support your self-confidence work:

1. Determine an area where you need to improve your confidence. Perhaps it's speaking up in groups or feeling better about your appearance.

2. Write down three positive affirmations to support this activity. For example, if your activity is speaking out in a meeting or group situation, an affirmation could be, "I calmly and confidently share my ideas in group settings, knowing that what I have to say has value. It is easy and natural for me to share my ideas in a group setting."

3. Whenever you feel resistance or have negative thoughts about your area of low confidence, repeat your affirmations out loud or say them silently to yourself. This will feel awkward at first, but you are training your brain to embrace this new behavior.

4. Also, take a few minutes twice a day to visualize yourself confidently performing this low confidence activity. Mentally reinforce the physical actions you want to take.

5. Continue to consistently practice affirming and visualizing yourself behaving confidently in this specific area. Adopting a new behavior requires repetition. Be patient with yourself as you wait for

your brain to adapt to your new behavior and your feelings of confidence around it.

Of course affirmations and visualization alone don't create confidence. You must put the confident behaviors into action. But they do add power to all of the confidence skills you're learning in this book. You can visualize and say affirmations any time of day to add muscle to your confidence. Understanding the way the brain works—how it is adaptable and dynamic—can give you faith to know with repetition, practice, and visualization, you can recreate yourself into a self-confident person.

As you grow in this "brain-trained" level of self-confidence, you'll have more enthusiasm and motivation to do more and achieve more, which in turn will provide a higher level of self-confidence. Basically, if you think and behave like the person you want to become, even if you have to fake it at first, eventually you will become that person.

Action Steps

In what area(s) do you need to work on your confidence? Begin to boost your confidence with some brain training work. Write down the specific problems you have with your confidence in this area. Then write three positive affirmations reflecting new confident behaviors.

Visualize yourself in detail performing confidently in this area, seeing how easy it is for you and how self-assured you feel. Several times a day, verbally or silently repeat your affirmations and practice the visualization.

Chapter 4:
Common Barriers to Confidence

IN THE FIRST chapters of this book, you learned more about confidence—what it is and how it manifests. Now we'll explore some of the reasons we lose our confidence and how low confidence is expressed in our behaviors, emotions, thoughts, and appearance. One of the first steps in understanding the source of low confidence is by identifying your confidence barriers, the places that trip you up when it comes to feeling good about your ability to succeed in a particular situation or in general. In order to solve a problem, you must first identify what it is.

Although every person's confidence barriers are specific to their personal life experiences and outlook, there are some common barriers that apply to everyone. Here are five of them:

Fear

The most common barrier to sustained self-confidence is fear. Perhaps you have a fear of failure, a fear rejection, or you may even have a fear of success. You might fear success because it sets the bar so high and comes with so many expectations and responsibilities. However, the vast majority of your fears are imaginary. The only place these fears exist are in your mind. Take a minute to think about your fears that undermine self-confidence. Are they truly grounded in any reality? Is there any evidence they will come to pass? Are you afraid of something that hasn't even happened or isn't likely to happen? Even if some part of your fear comes to pass, it's rarely as scary or debilitating as you fear it will be.

Worry and Overthinking

Another barrier to confidence is worry and thought looping. You might constantly think about appearing perfect, about what others think of you, or that you might make a mistake or fail at something. Worry can become circular, habitual thinking reinforced through mindless practice. Your brain latches on to a thought, and like a gerbil on a wheel, it's hard to let it go.

Worry and overthinking develop because you have a mindset that's far too focused on perceptions and superficial outcomes rather than on being who you are, living in the present moment, and accepting yourself. When you become engaged in action, through work or play, and when you do something to help or serve other people, you don't have time for worry. Your brain is too engaged in more important things. When you do have down time and find yourself in the worry cycle again, just say the word "stop" out loud to interrupt the worry thoughts. Then redirect your thinking to something positive, or engage your mind in reading, writing, helping someone, or creating.

Procrastination

Procrastination robs you of your confidence because it stealthily holds you down and keeps you from living to your potential. Every time you leave something undone or wait until the last minute, you will never perform as well as you could have. The outcome will never be as positive or productive. Procrastination makes you feel incapable, but in reality, all you need to do is begin. Taking the initiative to simply start something is generally the most difficult part.

Determine your priorities, give yourself plenty of time, and plan your tasks according to your priorities. If you find yourself moving a task to the bottom of the list repeatedly, make a point to put that task at the top and do it right away. It will only continue to drain you of emotional energy if you continue to put it off. Just start, take one small action, and it will carry you the rest of the way—boosting your confidence that you can take action the next time.

Indecision

The ability to make decisions, even when you aren't 100 percent sure, is essential for building confidence. Indecision can paralyze you and render you ineffective and insecure. You can change by giving yourself deadlines to make a decision and then sticking to it. Decisions rarely come with a guarantee, so you will always feel some risk with any decision. The challenge is getting comfortable with the discomfort of risk. Most decisions aren't permanent. You can change your decision if new information suggests amending it.

But waiting to make a decision until everything is perfect will immobilize you. The perfect time will never come, so pick a reasonable time and stick to it. It's better for your confidence to make a decision, even if it's ultimately the wrong one, than to make no decision at all. (I'll talk more about decision-making later in the book.)

Doubt

Doubt is often the sneaky culprit for all of the other four barriers. Your fear, worry thoughts, and indecisiveness arise from doubt in your own abilities, wisdom, and judgment. But if you don't believe in yourself, why should anyone else believe in you?

If you have a history of making poor decisions or using bad judgment, then examine what you learned from these situations and how you can change them going forward. Most of the time, this isn't the case. As adults, we have plenty of experience to afford us wisdom and discernment. We simply don't trust ourselves.

Who knows better what is best for you than you do? Begin to view yourself as someone with inner wisdom and self-knowledge. You have the answers inside of yourself, even if you don't trust those answers. You can turn doubt around by practicing small acts of self-trust. Pick a manageable situation where you doubt yourself or your abilities. Then proceed with your best judgment in spite of your doubts. Practice taking action even when you aren't sure. You'll be exercising your confidence muscle.

These common confidence barriers impact everyone. We all experience fear, worry, procrastination, indecision, and doubt from time to time. But when these feelings overwhelm our ability to achieve success, enjoy relationships, speak up, or make an income, then they need to be addressed and dismantled.

Action Steps

Do you see how these confidence barriers have impacted you in the past? You may find patterns of thoughts and behaviors related to one or more of these barriers that undermine your self-confidence. For each of the five common barriers, write down specific scenarios or life areas where they undermine your confidence.

Chapter 5:
Childhood Wounds, Adult Limitations

BEYOND THE COMMON emotional and mental barriers to confidence, there are other more deeply entrenched reasons we lose our way and stop believing in ourselves. We've trained ourselves to believe certain things over many, many years—perhaps dating back to childhood. If we felt unsupported, unloved, harshly criticized, or abused during our young years, our feelings of confidence and self-worth can be severely damaged. Having the security of loving, emotionally healthy, and fully present parents is essential to our own emotional and psychological health.

Over the years, any negative beliefs you may have about your abilities and worthiness have become so ingrained that you might not realize they're no longer true or necessary. And you probably don't comprehend how profoundly they hold you back from your potential. I'd bet ninety percent of the goals you wish to accomplish in life could be accomplished—if it weren't for limiting beliefs and the incredibly powerful feelings that fuel these beliefs. According to Jesuit priest, psychotherapist, and author Anthony de Mello, "There is only one cause of unhappiness: the false beliefs you have in your head, beliefs so widespread, so commonly held, that it never occurs to you to question them."

Consider what life would be like for you if all of those ancient beliefs about yourself simply disappeared. You are now a blank slate where all possibilities are valid options for you. There's nothing holding you back from being or trying anything. That's an empowering thought. Unfortunately, there are varying degrees of childhood pain that do hold us back—and all of us have some of these. Childhood issues that remain unresolved and untreated can infect your life and happiness throughout adulthood. They can impact your relationships profoundly, severely limiting your confidence in the one area that is vital to being whole.

The Teenage Years

Teenagers commonly suffer from confidence issues—it is part of what defines adolescence. As emerging adults, they struggle with their identity and place in the world. They look to their peers for reinforcement and positive feedback, but often receive harsh or even cruel responses to their longing for acceptance. Add a dose of acne, a weight problem, or anything perceived as slightly abnormal or unattractive, and you have the recipe for a teenage self-confidence implosion. Many of us look back on our teenage years the way war has been described—long stretches of tedium followed by moments of sheer terror.

Fortunately, most of us outgrow our teenage angst and awkwardness. Acne disappears, we know how to choose supportive friends, we encounter life successes along the way, and we aren't quite as self-absorbed. However, we carry the scars from our teenage years along with us as we grow. Even those who had happy, healthy upbringings have suffered some early hurts or insecurities that still linger into adulthood. An otherwise self-confident person might lack confidence in one particular area of their lives due to some early, relatively minor event. I'm sure you can remember one comment or experience from your youth that still stings and impacts how you feel about yourself. The more years we've had to reinforce those early beliefs about ourselves, the more ingrained the beliefs have become. In fact, sometimes we aren't even conscious of our limiting beliefs based on these early issues. We just respond in the way that feels automatic and safe, even if the beliefs are severely limiting us.

Some of these more serious childhood issues require the assistance of a professional counselor to help you move past the debilitating pain so you can embrace your self-worth and begin changing your thoughts and behaviors. With therapy you can gain insight into why you feel and act the way you do in life. You may also learn how certain triggers will cause you to react in childish or defensive ways that further damage healthy relationships and undermine self-confidence. And you might discover that you actually perpetuate the confidence-destroying words and actions you learned from parents or siblings. If you suffered serious emotional or physical trauma as a child, I strongly encourage you to work with a licensed professional therapist. That said, there are some actions you can begin today to start releasing limiting beliefs and boosting your self-confidence.

Addressing Limiting Beliefs

Take a moment and think about a negative, limiting belief you can trace back to a childhood or adolescent event or circumstance. If there are several, just pick one for now, perhaps the one that bothers or inhibits you most. For example, you might think, "I don't deserve a loving relationship." Or "I am bound to fail at whatever I try."

Next, think about the event or events back when you were younger you believe triggered those beliefs. Consider how the triggering events that happened years ago are no longer real for you in your current life. For example, you might say your parents no longer berate you, or the children at school no longer tease you. How has reality changed for you since those events? How have you moved past those triggering events?

Now think again about your limiting belief triggered by a childhood event or comment. What are some real facts that contradict that belief? For example, if you believe you aren't capable of success, consider the times you have been successful in recent weeks or years. Lastly, come up with a positive affirmation or statement that is the opposite of your limiting belief, such as, "I am capable of succeeding in any endeavor."

Here's a summary of what you've just done with this exercise:

1. You have shown how your current reality is different from the childhood issues that triggered your limiting belief.

2. You have undermined the truth of the limiting belief with contradictory evidence.

3. You've created an affirmative statement supporting the opposite of the limiting belief.

Now it's your job to put this exercise into practice when you notice a limiting belief arising for you. When you notice yourself thinking about or reacting to your limiting belief, force yourself to stop the thought pattern. You can even wear a rubber band on your wrist, and gently snap it to break the thinking pattern. Or just say, "Stop!" out loud or to yourself. Then replace the old thought with your new affirmation. An affirmation isn't just filler for the negative thoughts you've dropped. As discussed earlier, affirmations are powerful, brain-altering tools to support your confidence efforts.

Your past doesn't have to define your future. Most of the thoughts and feelings keeping you tethered to the status quo are simply that—thoughts and feelings. They have little or no substance in reality. Practice challenging your thoughts and create new, affirmative thoughts to replace these outdated limiting beliefs.

Action Steps

What are some of the limiting beliefs you've carried with you over the years? Write down those beliefs and follow the steps listed above to contradict them. Then write down the affirmation you created to read over again any time you struggle with your limiting belief.

With repeated practice of dropping negative thoughts, using positive affirmations, and taking positive actions, you can release the grip of outdated thoughts, change your thinking patterns, and begin to rebuild your confidence.

Chapter 6:
Mirror, Mirror—How Appearance Can Shatter Self-Assurance

IT'S HARD TO be attractive—and even harder to *feel* attractive. So much of our confidence, and for some people even their self-worth, is tied to appearance and how we perceive our appearance. Most of us simply aren't happy with how we look. It's no wonder we feel insecure. The current media ideal for women's overall appearance is achievable by less than two percent of the female population. Yet we are bombarded with this unrealistic ideal. Young women today see more images of exceptionally beautiful women in one day than our mothers saw throughout their entire teenage years. It's no wonder eight out of ten women are dissatisfied with their appearance.

The truth is that most of us aren't "beautiful" by the current media standards. Even models and actresses are outed as less than perfect when they're caught in their natural state by lurking tabloid photographers. Maintaining that standard of perfection must be exhausting and humiliating. This focus on physical attractiveness isn't just a female issue. Surprisingly men worry as much or more about their body shape and appearance than women do. According to a study from the Center of Appearance Research at the University of the West of England, more than four in five men (80.7 percent) talk in ways that promote anxiety about their body image by referring to perceived flaws and imperfections, compared with 75 percent of women. And 38 percent of men would sacrifice at least a year of their life in exchange for a perfect body—again, a higher proportion than women.

Says Dr. Phillippa Diedrichs, from the Center, "These findings tell us that men are concerned about body image, just like women. We knew that 'body talk' affected women and young people and now we know that it affects men too." Dr. Diedrichs conducted the study of 394 British men, which was commissioned by Central YMCA and the Succeed Foundation, an eating disorders charity. The study revealed how men have high levels of anxiety about their bodies and that some resort to compulsive exercise, strict diets, laxatives or making themselves sick in an attempt to lose weight or achieve a more toned physique.

Even though we know this standard of physical perfection is unrealistic and unattainable, most of us spend far too much time, emotional energy, and money attempting to keep up. It doesn't matter whether you're young with enviable skin and a tight butt or beginning to see gray hairs and wrinkles, you likely focus more on your perceived flaws than you do on any aspect of your true attractiveness. Although attractiveness can help you get a foot in the door, it has very little to do with sustaining relationships, success on the job, and even less with developing real confidence. We've all seen beautiful people who open their mouths and become instantly less attractive, or unattractive people who become more appealing because they exude something special.

Wouldn't it be wonderful to wave a magic wand and eliminate all of the insecurities and self-loathing wrapped up in the struggle to be attractive enough? What if you could walk away from it all and live your life focused on what makes you joyful and confident? From the time we become aware of our appearance (somewhere during that pre-teen awkwardness), we have a love-hate relationship with our faces and bodies. We learn societal standards of attractiveness and begin to recognize how we fall short.

Think of all of the pain and unhappiness your face and body image has caused you over the years. If there's a flaw, you search it out like a heat seeking missile and obsess about it until that's all you see. It's perplexing to hear beautiful models or actors talk about their gawky teen years and how they hated their appearance. This self-image often carries over into their adult self-perceptions, in spite of their obvious good looks. Even beautiful people lack confidence about their appearance.

It's often those same beautiful models and actors who reinforce our negative self-image when we see them in magazines, movies, or on TV. Perfection is everywhere in the media, but in life we are all existing in imperfect bodies that are flawed, flabby, and forever aging. That is a reality, and though we may fight against it, our bodies and faces do have minds of their own.

Confidence vs. Beauty

Men and women alike find confidence in the opposite sex one of the most attractive qualities. Several studies and surveys in both men and women have indicated that confidence and high self-esteem are most admirable in members of the complementary sex.

American love expert Ellen Kriedman, PhD, lists confidence as number one of the top fifteen turn-on's for women in her book, *The 10 Second Kiss*. Other polls have shown men are similarly attracted to females who have self-esteem, confidence and independence. Confidence is seen in how you walk, talk, dress and your attitude toward yourself and others. This is good news for those of us who will never make it on the pages of a magazine (and that's most of us). We can feel more self-confident, attractive, and accepting of our physicality by shifting our focus and attitude. There is another way to relate to your appearance, one that reinforces self-acceptance. Here are some thoughts:

- Begin to adopt a more spiritual approach to your relationship with your face and body.

- Bless your body daily for all of the amazing ways it supports you.

- View your body and appearance as a sacred garment housing your unique self and treat it with loving kindness.

When we begin to see our bodies as a wondrous gift, even with all of its flaws, we can live in harmony with it rather than resisting and hating it. Here are some thoughts on how to create a new relationship with your appearance in order to support your confidence work.

Give Up Resistance

When we resist and struggle, we are expending mental and emotional energy that is depleting. This struggle never serves to make things better, even though we believe we can out-think our difficulties and issues. Accept the reality of what is—being overweight, wrinkly, too short, too tall, having an average appearance, whatever. This is who you are right now, so allow your mind and heart to rest peacefully in that for now.

Shift Your Perceptions

View your body and face as a beloved friend with whom you have a sacred relationship. This friend has been with you since you were born and will be with you until the end. This friend has carried you thousands of miles, has kept you nourished, and has functioned reliably most of the time. This friend knows what to do when it comes to sustaining, healing, and reproducing. It has given you indescribable pleasures and yes, some pain too. However, we haven't always been kind to our body-friend. We have caused it pain and betrayed it in a variety of ways, so now it's time to be a good and loving friend to your body and face.

45

Be Mindful

Our bodies may be flawed, but we shouldn't reprimand or belittle them. In fact, acknowledge the aesthetic of your body. Look at the beauty and wisdom in your eyes, and see how fluidly your limbs move, support, and carry you. Look at your hands and how they speak of the loving touch, the meals prepared, and the work done over the years. Your heart is pumping blood, your lungs are taking in oxygen, and your digestive system works to nourish your body and rid it of waste. All of the organs and systems are working in beautiful harmony to sustain you. There is so much more beauty than ugliness if you shift your perception.

Take Tender Care

As you acknowledge all your body has does for you, your resistance will soften, and you'll see what a miracle your body is. It may not be perfect or perfectly appealing to the mass media, but even with its flaws, it is working superbly. Treat it well and lovingly so it can continue to serve you.

- Feed your body with whole, nutritious foods.

- Hydrate it with pure, clean water.

- Listen to what your body needs for nutrition.

- Educate yourself about healthy eating if you aren't sure.

- Regard everything you put in your mouth, and ask yourself, "Is this showing love to my body?"

- Move your body to keep it flexible, to stimulate your internal organs, to maintain a weight that doesn't stress your system, and to relieve stress and toxins.

- Create a habit of regular exercise that is simple, fun, and moderately challenging.

- Give up habits that are harmful to your body, like smoking, over-eating or drinking, harmful drugs, or tanning.

- Protect your body by not putting it in danger. Wear seat belts, helmets, and sunscreen, and put down your cell phone when driving.

- Care for your body by getting regular check-ups and seeking timely medical attention when you suspect you need it.

- Give peace to your body by dealing with stress through meditation, creativity, relaxation, and movement.

Love Your Flaws

We have grown to hate our body flaws because they reflect our fears—our fears of aging and death, rejection, failure, and ugliness. Begin to make a conscious effort to love your flaws, as strange as this might sound.

Love your humanness.

Love the years of living and experiences your flaws reveal.

Love the peace that being imperfect offers.

Love your connection to a world of flawed people.

Love the lack of control you have over some of your flaws.

Being flawed is essential to our humanity. Love that.

Embrace the sacredness

View your body as the sacred garment of your inner self. When you embrace it in this light, it's difficult to reject and shame it. In fact, you will begin to respect your face and body and love them for all of their glorious beauty and function. Become conscious of your actions and behaviors and how they affect your body. Seen in this new light, your body will transform from the inside out. You will not have to struggle against it—you will work with it and find it responds to your love in a myriad of positive ways, including feeling more relaxed and confident.

Action Steps

How attractive do you feel relative to other men or women your age? On a scale of one to ten, with ten being extremely attractive and one being extremely unattractive, how would you rate yourself?

What has impacted you most related to your self-image about your appearance? (i.e., your parents' comments, friends' comments, the media, etc.) What are your feelings now about these sources of influence? Do they still hold impact for you? How are their messages untrue?

What do you think are your best physical qualities? What parts of your inner-self do you feel are most attractive or beautiful?

How can you be kinder to yourself related to your appearance? What positive thoughts can you substitute for your negative thoughts about your appearance?

Chapter 7:
People Pleasing and Perfectionism

WHAT DO OUR culture, the mass media, and those close to you tell you about who you should be and how you should live? What pressure do you feel to make other people happy and to live up to their expectations? Wafting around us all the time are subtle and not-so-subtle messages reminding us of what it takes to measure up and fit in. Measuring up boils down to a very basic human need—to be loved and accepted. We strive to fit in because we don't want to be left out.

We all crave love and acceptance, but from a young age, we're trained to believe it hinges on the approval of other people.

- If we obey our parents and are good boys and girls, we win their hugs, kind words, and praise.

- If we perform well in school, we're rewarded with the teacher's accolades and the respect of fellow students.

- If we dress the right way and look attractive, we're rewarded with attention and romance.

- If we grow up, get the right job, and make a lot of money, we win the respect and envy of our peers and inclusion into best circles.

None of these pursuits are wrong. In fact many of them can provide us with some amount of confidence. But they can *become* wrong if we put the cart before the horse. These pursuits become debilitating if we're driven to pursue them primarily by the need for approval and acceptance. When we define ourselves and our actions by "I should" rather than "I want" or "I am," we're building a house with no foundation. We set ourselves up to be swayed by the capricious demands and desires of everyone around us.

The Messages around Us

Granted, it's hard not to be impacted by pressures and expectations. The media attempts to brainwash us, not only related to appearance, but in all areas of our lives. To be worthy and lovable, we must be young and attractive, live in a spacious and well-decorated home, drive a sexy car, have the perfect mate and kids, and make enough money to afford all of these things. In addition, there are people shouting at us about our political views, what our religious beliefs should be, what kind of food we should eat, how we should raise our children, and how we should spend our free time. Even if we could block out the extraneous noise from society telling us who we should be and what we should do, we often have family and friends offering up their expectations for us.

If you were raised in a family where love hinged on towing the line, being compliant, and responding to guilt trips, you may be deeply entrenched in the quicksand of "should." There are parents of adult children who still control and manipulate to get what they want, and there are many adult children who facilitate this behavior by responding to it for fear of rejection. The need for constant approval also can result from an overdeveloped fear of failure. This fear often is a response to early experiences of criticism or harsh judgment when you made a mistake as a child. Even if the critical adult is no longer in your life, the anxiety and need to please remain. To cope with this anxiety, we do everything we can to be perfect and ensure everyone is happy.

According to transformational psychologist and author Jay Early, PhD, if you're a people pleaser, you "often try to be who others want you to be, to agree with them, to fit in. You may not be consciously aware that you are doing this, but there is a part of your psyche that wants to please others in order to avoid reactions that you are afraid of."

Here are some of the behaviors Dr. Early suggests are common to people pleasers:

- I try to be who someone wants me to be.

- I am afraid to rock the boat.

- It is hard for me to know what I want.

- I avoid speaking my mind.

- I find it easier to go along with what someone wants or with their opinion.

- I fantasize about a strong person taking over my life and making it work.

- It is hard for me to express my feelings when they are different from someone I'm close to.

- It is difficult for me to say "No."

- I avoid getting angry.

- It is hard for me to take initiative.

- I try to be nice rather than expressing how I really feel.

- I want everyone to get along.

Author and coach Steve Chandler reminds in his book *Time Warrior*,

> If I've trained myself throughout my life to place my highest survival value on being non-threatening, accommodating, not making waves, not standing out, being like everyone else—then that becomes the belief system I take into adulthood. How could it not be?

He suggests that sadly, "most people stay stuck in a version of childhood forever." So how do we become self-confident grown-ups? How do we change our belief system and step out of the cycle of perfectionism, expectations and shoulds?

The Way Forward

The very first step is getting to know yourself again—or maybe for the first time. Start by looking at every single area of your life and asking, "Is this really me? Is this who I am, what I want to be doing, how I want to live?" If you have spent years morphing into a person defined by others, then the real you may be hidden and unknown. It's your job to find and define that person—if you're going to find true and sustainable self-confidence. In doing so, you must accept there will be some discomfort. Reclaiming your true self might mean you offend some people, make someone angry or frustrated, or go against expectations. This is extremely disconcerting for a people pleaser who lacks confidence and is addicted to approval.

With practice however, you'll learn to tolerate disapproval or anger as you create your own personal boundaries. In fact, as you develop in confidence, you'll become more and more immune to the bad behavior of those who previously sought to control or manipulate you. You'll relax and feel less driven to be perfect and perfectly accommodating. As Dr. Early encourages, experiment with asserting your autonomy. Work on knowing what you think, feel, and want, even when it is different from other people. He suggests you practice the following behaviors.

- Set limits when you need to.

- Express your desires or opinions.

- Stand your ground when others disagree or push their perspective.

- Recognize that other people may not always like what you say or do, and take the risk to do it anyway.

As you practice being autonomous, your inner people pleaser may fear you are being unpleasant or unnecessarily aggressive because you aren't accustomed to standing your ground. Reassure the people pleaser that you're simply taking care of yourself, and it's essential and healthy to do so.

Making decisions, choices, and actions based on winning love and approval is a throwback to childish needs and insecurities—when Mom and Dad held all the cards and power. Now you're an adult, and you can make choices to please yourself, even if it means offending someone else. You can certainly *make the decision* to please or accommodate, but this choice should be made from a place of power and love, not insecure need. Authentic love and approval begins with approving of yourself and embracing what is true for you. Once you do that, other people who see you as you are, will be naturally drawn to you.

Action Steps

In what areas of your life do you feel you are people-pleasing, accommodating, or living up to expectations against your authentic self? What do you gain by people-pleasing? What specific feelings, payback, or comfort do you derive from it?

Think about the areas of your life where people pleasing is particularly problematic for you. If you could be the person you wanted to be in these areas, who would that person be and how would you behave differently?

Barrie Davenport

Chapter 8:
The Confidence Myths
Holding You Back

ASSUME FOR A moment a situation exists that's uncomfortable or possibly painful for you. If you had the choice of knowing or not knowing the painful truth about it, which would you choose? If shining the spotlight on an area of your life might open a can of worms and cause immediate complications, would you rather take a good hard look or keep that area in darkness? Facing the truth about certain things in life is not fun. Most of us prefer to pull the covers over our heads, and put our fingers in our ears. It is far easier than facing the difficult or painful truth. Or is it?

Like most of us, you likely experienced family lies and pretense when you were growing up that were perpetuated by mutual consent. Grandpa's drinking problem was never discussed. Parental conflict was inflicted on you but never explained or addressed. Mom pretended she was happy but always looked sad. You can fill in your own version of this failure to face reality or to gloss over the unpleasant things in life, and these glossed over scenarios can do a number on our confidence. When we can't be honest with ourselves or others, when there are big secrets and little lies, how can we feel open and confident about who we are?

We learn from these early family experiences that painful or difficult things should be left alone—that the appropriate response for something uncomfortable is to pretend it doesn't exist or to quickly sweep it under the rug. Basically, we learn to lie—to ourselves and to others. On the surface, avoidance and denial don't seem as deceitful as overtly lying. Lying is intentional and done with full awareness. Avoidance and denial are more acts of omission and self-preservation. But if we're being completely real, most of the time we know we're lying to ourselves and burying our heads in the sand.

The unfortunate truth about lying to yourself is that it's only a temporary fix. Self-deception is the finger in the dam that keeps you firmly positioned in one spot so everything around you doesn't come crashing down. Eventually those deceptions spill over into all areas of our lives—our thoughts about ourselves, our relationships, our beliefs, and our general perceptions of the world around us. The line between what is real and true becomes blurred with what we want to be real and true—so we pretend.

Self-deception may feel easy and safe at first, but eventually it cripples you and sabotages your confidence. These lies prevent you from seeing things clearly, living life fully, and evolving into the person you want to be. Even though you do your best to maintain these deceptions, they have a way of springing leaks and causing unpleasant symptoms.

Self-deception can cause . . .

- anxiety

- depression

- low self-esteem

- low motivation

- lack of focus

- poor relationships

- job difficulties

- over-spending

- physical ailments

There are some core myths we tell ourselves that perpetuate self-deception and have a huge negative impact on our confidence. These are the lies that touch virtually every aspect of our being and create a cascade of smaller deceptions that serve the larger master. Here are ten common myths that will sabotage your self-confidence:

1. I'm not good enough.

This is a story we've all told ourselves and others at some point in life, and it boils down to feeling unlovable. We may have valid reasons for feeling this way on occasion, and some people have had tragic life events that reinforce this feeling. The problem arises when you start to really believe it, and you bolster the myth with words and actions.

The Truth: No matter what you've done, what you've experienced, or how you might feel, you are good enough. You are lovable. There is no universal measuring stick for "good enough." The only requirement for lovability is to be yourself and accept yourself, and fortunately the right people will be attracted to your authenticity. Stop using negative words or thoughts about yourself. Replace those with all of the reasons you are lovable and worthy. Write them down, speak them, and continue to define who you are in your best vision for yourself.

2. I can't do that.

The sub-themes of this deception include I'm Too Old, It's Too Late, I'm Not Smart Enough, and It Won't Work. Our fallback story when presented with an opportunity or challenge is, "I can't do that." Maybe you can't—but you probably can, and you won't know unless you try.

The Truth: It may take some creative thinking, some hard work, some sacrifice, but you can (almost always) do it if you choose too. Rather than beginning with a negative assumption, intend that you can do it until proven otherwise. Change your mindset to expect the positive rather than the negative.

3. My beliefs are right.

Really? Says who? There is another side to every belief you have—positive or negative beliefs. You may believe yourself to be incapable, but there's plenty of evidence to the contrary, so find it. You may believe you hold the correct point of view—but so does that other guy. Listen to him, and consider his truth.

The Truth: Your beliefs are not 100 percent true. In fact some of them may not be true at all. Write down some of the beliefs you have about yourself and about the world around you. Open your mind to contradictions to your belief. Allow yourself to shift your thinking when you are exposed to truth. Accepting a new truth can be painful and scary, but it's far better than living a lie.

4. I know best.

This ties in with assumptions about our beliefs. We think we know best how others should think, behave, and respond to us. We want people to change and accommodate our vision of who they should be. We believe our desires would be best for everyone. Often we do this because what we dislike in others is something we don't like in ourselves.

The Truth: Expecting others to change is a huge self-deception and can foster low self-esteem. People may try to accommodate you, but real change will never really happen, and then they'll resent you. You'll never have an authentic relationship and will ultimately feel bad about yourself and your ability to sustain relationships. Acknowledge and accept that those you love are fine just as they are. They are flawed and different than you, but that makes them real and interesting. Open your eyes to the truth about who they really are, and allow them to safely be that person.

5. Mediocre is fine with me.

If you just keep telling yourself this, maybe you'll believe it. Why step up to your potential when it takes so much time and energy? It's too hard, too much work. It's fine to stay comfortable just where you are, but what is this doing to your confidence?

The Truth: Mediocre isn't fine. Your higher self will keep nagging at you, making life miserable until you step up to the plate and do something. You know you don't want to settle for a compromised life. What part of your life are you allowing to remain mediocre? What does your higher self want you to do instead? What are you willing to do today to get the ball rolling on this?

6. I don't have time.

I would do that thing if I only had time. I would try that new habit, follow my passion, work on my relationship, spend time with my children—if I only had time.

The Truth: Time is yours to manipulate as you wish. There isn't an endless supply of it, but there's plenty to create a life around what is most important to you. It's all about prioritizing choices. Procrastination and avoidance drag you down and undermine your feelings of productivity and control. What are your top five priorities in life? Where are you wasting time on meaningless things? Remove the non-essentials, and manipulate time around the priorities.

7. I can live with that.

A cluttered house. A rude friend. A spouse who belittles you. Children who talk back. People who interrupt your time. Tedious tasks that find their way to the forefront. You can live with these, right? They aren't such a big deal.

The Truth: People and things you are merely tolerating are slowly sucking your energy and joy. When you roll over and allow people to walk all over you, you lose self-respect. You lose dignity. And you lose confidence in your standards. What are you putting up with that is draining you? What people are crossing your boundaries? What are you willing to do about it?

8. Once this happens, then I'll be happy.

How has that deception worked for you so far? I'll be happy when I find the right spouse. I'll be happy when I get a promotion. I'll be happy when we have more money. It will just take a little more time, a little more effort—then I'll be happy.

The Truth: Pinning happiness on a future event is like trying to capture a runaway kitten. Just when you think you have it in your hands, it slips away from your grasp, beckoning you forward forever. The best isn't yet to come, it's right now. Happiness is always at hand and can be found in this moment alone. Look for happiness in who you are and what you are doing right now. Even if you aren't feeling your most self-confident, shift your focus away from your bad feelings and focus on the task at hand.

9. Failure isn't an option.

I can't fail because I have a standard to live up to. I can't fail because people will think I'm a loser. I can't fail because it will announce to the world that I'm not who I say I am. Failure isn't an option—I must do everything in my power not to fail, including not trying.

The Truth: If you want to grow, succeed, and achieve things, then failure must be an option. Failure is evidence of effort and action. Failure is a necessary teacher available to serve you, not harm you. Look at past failures that have caused you pain. What have you learned from them that's helped you grow and make changes? How can you begin to embrace failure and view it as less of a threat?

10. It isn't my fault.

It isn't my fault I'm not successful—I had a difficult childhood. It isn't my fault I'm unhappy because I hate my job. It isn't my fault that people don't like me. They just don't understand my personality.

The Truth: As adults, we're fully responsible for our actions, circumstances, and relationships. If we had past hurts or tragedy, it is our responsibility to ourselves and our loved ones to seek help. If we're unhappy, it's our responsibility to find the cause of our unhappiness and do something about it. Where do you have a belief that it is not your fault? How can you take full ownership and responsibility for this situation, and what can you do about it?

Facing the truth about these personal lies can be painful, but it's like pulling off a band-aid. The sting will subside, the wound will heal, and you will have the freedom to experience a fuller life empowered by reality. Acknowledging the truth will lift a weight off of you, releasing you from the crippling restraints of self-deception and allowing you to move forward with confidence.

Action Steps

Review the ten myths that hamper your confidence. Which of these myths apply to you and your beliefs about yourself? What actions do you need to take to bust these myths in order to free yourself for confidence? Write down some specific actions you're willing to take in the next few weeks to embrace the truth in these situations.

Chapter 9:
Social Shyness and Fear of Speaking

LOW CONFIDENCE OFTEN is the result of some form of social shyness. "Shyness," according to *Psychology Today*'s definition, "is the awkwardness or apprehension some people feel when approaching or being approached by other people." Unlike introverts who feel energized by time alone, shy people often desperately want to connect with others, but don't know how or can't tolerate the anxiety that comes with social interaction. Do you recognize yourself at socially shy? If so, you aren't alone. Nearly half of all Americans claim to be shy, and it appears a shyness epidemic is on the rise. Technology is contributing to this surge in shyness, as more and more people can hide behind their computers and avoid face-to-face interactions.

Even moderately shy people now have an excuse to avoid social interactions and new situations. All they need for company and companionship is at the push of a button. The diminishing opportunities for face-to-face communication in personal and professional life put shy people at an increasing disadvantage, as they don't get to practice social skills within the comfort of daily routines. Even before the popularity of online socializing and cyber connections, shyness was a surprisingly common issue among many Americans, and even more common in other cultures like Japan and Taiwan.

In 1975, Stanford University psychologist Philip Zimbardo, PhD, wrote an article for *Psychology Today* entitled "The Social Disease Called Shyness." The article underscored the pervasiveness of shyness, with forty percent of the 800 people questioned stating they were shy. What's even more surprising is that many of self-described shy people don't appear shy at all to others. Recent studies on shyness suggest most shyness is hidden from others. In fact, only a small percentage of shy people, about fifteen to twenty percent, appear to be obviously ill at ease—but all suffer internally.

Says Dr. Bernado Carducci, director of the Indiana University Southeast Shyness Research Institute,

> Their mild-mannered exterior conceals roiling turmoil inside. The shy disclosed that they are excessively self-conscious, constantly sizing themselves up negatively, and overwhelmingly preoccupied with what others think of them. While everyone else is meeting and greeting, they are developing plans to manage their public impression.

The majority of shy people spend agonizing amounts of time and energy trying to hide their shyness. While they may seem comfortable and confident in social settings, they're often engaging in a negative and self-defeating inner dialogue, feeling awkward, insecure, and questioning how they're being viewed or judged by others.

Shyness, whether concealed or obvious, wreaks internal havoc for those who experience it. They encounter social problems like difficulty meeting people and making new friends, which may lead to isolation, loneliness, and depression. Their reserve in conversation may lead others to believe they're snobbish or disinterested when really they're just plain nervous. Shy people are incessantly preoccupied with their appearance and behavior, feeling acutely self-conscious. They're caught between the fear of being invisible and insignificant to others, and the fear of being visible but feeling worthless.

There are a wide variety of causes of social shyness in adults. These include one's culture (Westerners tend to be less shy in general than many Eastern cultures), as well as parenting styles and bonding, temperament, heredity, and life experiences. Regardless of the cause, however, most issues with shyness can be managed and overcome. A good place to start is with self-awareness and understanding *how* you are shy. Think about the situations that make you feel shy, such as meeting new people, being in social gatherings, or talking to a potential romantic partner. How does your shyness manifest—internally through self-consciousness and anxiety, or in your behavior such as your posture, loss of words, or withdrawal from others?

If you experience internal and physical symptoms of anxiety as part of your shyness, relaxation techniques such as conscious breathing can help bring the symptoms under control. You must be mostly free of anxiety symptoms in order to begin new, more confident behaviors. Simply understanding yourself and the way shyness affects your confidence can help you begin to address the problem. In social situations, there are several techniques you can try to help overcome shyness and rebuild your confidence

1. Start with small and non-threatening situations.

These might include malls, museums, or events where you can interact with a lot of people for a brief period of time. You can begin practicing social engagement by smiling and saying "hello" to as many people as you can. Ask someone for the time, or offer a compliment or assistance to someone. Find simple ways to practice talking with people. Manageable exposure to intimidating situations will slowly help you overcome your fears.

2. Practice conversational skills.

Have several topics ready to talk about with people you meet—perhaps a current news event or a comment about the surroundings. Ask open-ended questions and follow-up with comments about the person's answers. You can even practice some of these topics by yourself before you're in the situation.

3. Remember most people aren't really that focused on you.

People are far more interested in their own appearance and conversation. They aren't nearly as focused on your social skills or lack thereof as much as you fear. That reality alone should relieve some of your angst and discomfort.

4. Make a point of seeing what you've done well.

After a social interaction, rather than latching on to your perceived flaws and flubs, focus on what you did well in the situation, how you overcame a shy moment and felt confident. With practice, you will have more and more successes.

5. Create realistic expectations.

Many shy people hold themselves up to impossible standards of perfection when it comes to social situations. When they fall short, they're highly self-critical. You don't have to be the life of the party in order to have a successful interaction with people. Create realistic goals for yourself before you embark on a social situation.

6. Accept that some rejection is normal.

Everyone, whether or not they are shy, experiences some form of rejection by others from time to time. Not everyone will like you, and that's okay. Manage your expectations in this regard as well. More often than not, rejection has nothing to do with the person being rejected. Your goal is to make regular attempts to socialize with others and realize some will work out and some won't. Focus on the interactions that work.

If you suffer from low self-confidence in social situations and experience a level of shyness preventing you from enjoying being with other people, begin to take small and manageable actions to address the issue. Every small success will lead to incremental improvements in your confidence. Don't hide behind your computer, make excuses for not attending events, or avoid meeting new people. You're only holding yourself back from potential relationships that could bring you joy and expand your horizons. Engage in life by reconnecting with real people, and allow others to experience all of the gifts you have to offer.

Action Steps

What situations seem to make you feel shy? These might include meeting new people, being in social gatherings, or talking to a potential romantic partner. What are some small and non-threatening actions you are willing to take to challenge your shyness and stretch yourself?

Chapter 10:
Creating Your POS

AS I MENTIONED earlier, people with low confidence almost always look outside of themselves for affirmation and reinforcement. They look outside of themselves to find a blueprint for how to conduct their lives, how to think, and how to feel. This is different from looking to mentors or role models to inspire and guide you, or to coaches and counselors to help you move forward. When your confidence is low, you look to others to approve you, to prop you up, to give permission, or sanction your behavior. When you do this too often, it begins to impact your self-esteem as well.

By seeking this reinforcement, we revert back to the behaviors of childhood when our parents had to help us define and approve our choices and behaviors. As adults, this need for outside approval is no longer necessary. In fact, it's counter-productive, making us dependent on others for our well-being and happiness while relinquishing our personal power. Though we certainly don't want to give away our power, often we simply don't know how to claim it. We live unconsciously, on autopilot, not aware we have the power to create our lives proactively. We react to whatever happens to come our way, and haven't taken the time to define who we are and what we want from life. Some might believe they don't even have the choice to define this for themselves, feeling obligated to live a life defined by other people.

Creating Your Own POS: Personal Operating System

Deep inside every person is the profound longing to live authentically—to live the life we define for ourselves. We may not consciously understand that longing, but if this need is not met, our pain and longing come out in unhealthy ways—through depression, anger, anxiety, passive aggressive behaviors, and physical illness. In previous chapters, we've explored how you may be deceiving yourself and accepting lies that hold you back. We've looked at the roles you've assumed that may not be part of your authentic self. But now let's dig deeper to think about how you can proactively define your own POS—your personal operating system for your life.

Your POS is your worldview, your life orientation—how you consciously define your world and choose to operate within it. When we lack confidence, our prevailing operating system is a problem-focused, anxiety-based, and reactive way of being. Living in an often hostile and pain-oriented world, human beings honed the "fight, flight, or freeze" reaction to life experience. We are in a state of responding and reacting rather than creating. When you design your POS, you are empowering yourself for a new and more dynamic life orientation that isn't fear-based. You develop a set of authentic choices and actions for meeting life experience more effectively, creatively, and with much greater fulfillment and purpose.

So let's talk about how you can begin to create your own personal operating system. A POS is not something that can be achieved overnight, as it involves redesigning all areas of your life. But simply the knowledge that *you can* create your own personal operating system is hugely empowering and opens your eyes to how you are living unconsciously or allowing others to define your life for you. Right now, in this very moment, start to think about how you might change everything in your life if you had a chance for a do-over. Not that you *will* change everything. There are plenty of things working well in your life. But shift your mental orientation to the awareness that YOU have the power to recreate and begin again with many of your choices, beliefs, actions, and relationships.

Creating your personal operating system requires you examine every area of your life to determine whether or not it's in alignment with your desires, beliefs, and preferences. You won't be able to change everything, at least not right away, but you can change enough to boost your self-confidence tremendously. With every step and every act of self-creation, you are moving closer to the real you and building a foundation of confidence that will grow over time.

A great place to begin creating your POS is by defining your core values. Once you assess your values and define the most important values for your life and your career, you can use those values as the ballast for every decision involved in creating your POS. Your values are your guiding life principles and will provide the self-awareness to know how to behave and make decisions in all facets of your life—and this is incredibly empowering. As you shift toward your own POS, these values will keep you on track and motivate you when you have difficult choices or changes to make.

Living a life defined by your personal values and within your own personal operating systems means you are living consciously. You are living purposefully. The structure of having values and a well-considered POS immediately boosts your confidence, because you've built an authentic foundation for all of your choices and actions.

Action Steps

Clarify the top five or six core values for your life. You can review a list of 400 values words to help you. Access the words at http://www.barriedavenport.com/list-of-400-values/.

Then list the following areas of your life, leaving room to write beneath each:

- relationship

- career

- health

- learning and skill

- integrity

- money

- parenting

- other

Under each area, write down how you are operating outside of your values in this area or simply not living consciously and proactively. Then write the changes you'd like to make, the new operating system in each of these areas. Be sure your new operating system supports your values.

Barrie Davenport

Chapter 11:
Your Body Speaks Volumes

DEFINING HOW YOU want to live through your personal operating system is a great foundation for boosting confidence. But let's go back to our bodies and brains for a moment. Let's look at how you might be perpetuating low confidence, even with a solid POS, by using the wrong body language. The next time you're in a conversation with someone or at a meeting, pay attention to your body language. What does it say to others about your confidence and abilities? What is it reinforcing inside of you?

Our body language is a form of communication that speaks volumes about who we are and how we feel. You've likely encountered people whose mere presence sends a loud and clear message that they're on top of their game, full of confidence, and poise. On the other hand, you've seen people who walk into a room and fade into the background. Everything about them screams shy or uncomfortable.

Social psychologist Amy Cuddy in her popular TED presentation on body language, points out the powerful impact this non-verbal language has on the perceptions of those around us—right from the moment we meet them. She reminds,

> So social scientists have spent a lot of time looking at the effects of our body language, or other people's body language, on judgments. And we make sweeping judgments and inferences from body language. And those judgments can predict really meaningful life outcomes like who we hire or promote, who we ask out on a date.

Something as simple as how you hold your arms, where your eyes go, or the tilt of your head can make the difference in success or failure, a yes or a no, a dream fulfilled or never realized. Our body language sends immediate and powerful signals to others before they have a chance to say hello.

Alexander Todorov, a psychologist and professor at Princeton, has shown just how powerful body language can be in the world of politics. Through his research, he's proven that quick facial judgments can accurately predict real-world election returns. Todorov's lab tests showed how a brief appraisal of two candidates' faces and their relative competence was enough to predict the winner in about seventy percent of U.S. senate and state gubernatorial races in the 2006 elections. It only took about a tenth of a second. "We never told our test subjects they were looking at candidates for political office—we only asked them to make a gut reaction response as to which unfamiliar face appeared more competent," said Todorov. "The findings suggest that fast, unreflective judgments based on a candidate's face can affect voting decisions."

But what does our own body language do to us? If body language has such a profound and instantaneous impact on those who encounter us, imagine the cumulative effect of the messages we send ourselves. If you're head is bowed, your eyes averted, your arms crossed defensively, your shoulders slumped, and your feet are shuffling, consider what you're reinforcing in your neural pathways. "I am small, insignificant, shy, unworthy, unimportant." That is what your brain is hearing.

So what is the body language of confidence? It's expansive. It puffs up. It takes up space. It's literally larger than life. It's about stretching and expanding your body to take up as much space as possible. And most importantly, it can be reverse engineered. You don't have to feel confident to practice confident body language. In fact, practicing confident body language actually improves your feelings of confidence. Again, it's all about the messages you're sending to your brain. If you slump, avoid eye contact, and draw in, you are training your brain to embrace low confidence. However, if you practice confident body language, your feelings will eventually catch up.

In her research on body language, Amy Cuddy found that people who practice "high power" poses just for two minutes had a twenty percent increase in the dominance hormone testosterone and a twenty-five percent decrease in cortisol, the stress hormone. Those who display "low power" poses had a ten percent decrease in testosterone and a fifteen percent increase in cortisol. She also found that the high power posers were more likely to take risk than the low power posers, and risk-taking is associated with confidence.

A great way to begin using your body language to build your confidence is simply by becoming aware of your current body language. Pay attention as you enter a room, talk with someone new, or have a meeting with your boss. When you notice you're feeling uncomfortable or lacking confidence, stop and notice your body. Where are your arms and legs positioned? How are you holding your shoulders? What are you doing with your eyes? How often are you smiling? You can begin to make subtle changes as you notice what your body is telling others and reinforcing in yourself. In addition, you can practice power poses by yourself and in specific situations to boost your confidence.

Here are some poses Amy Cuddy recommends you try:

V for Victory

Before an interview or big meeting or whenever you want a surge of confidence, hold your arms in the air in a V position with clenched fists. Tilt your chin up, smile, and puff out your chest. Hold this position for two or three minutes.

The Mr. Clean

Even though crossed arms can communicate defensiveness, there are some situations to use it for power.

It's the position of your shoulders that's key. If you're trying to make a point or appear decisive and strong, hold your shoulders back with your arms crossed and head held high.

The Loomer

If you want to close the deal, win the case, convince someone of something, and command the room with your presence, lean forward while standing with your hands spread out on the table or desk and your feet slightly apart.

The Kick-Back

If you want to take more profitable risks, feel strong in pitching an idea, and more at ease in brainstorming, put your hands behind your head, lean back, and rest your feet on the table or desk. Obviously this won't work in all settings, but just practicing it can help you feel it and tap into those feelings when you need them.

The CEO

Lean back in your chair while resting one arm on the back of the chair. Open your chest and widen your shoulders. For guys, have your feet and legs slightly apart. The key is a wide open position that appears comfortable. You could also place your hands behind your head and an ankle on one knee. This is a strong position for interviewing someone, or appearing in command of the room.

The Wonder Woman

This is the classic hero figure pose with hands on hips, chest out, and feet planted hip width apart. It communicates confidence, strength, and poise. Try this power pose with your boss or anyone in authority to gain more respect and impact.

The Smile

Studies have shown just smiling alone is enough to boost your feelings of confidence and happiness. You don't need to feel happy or confident to practice smiling. Just smile in the mirror or when you're alone, and you're sending signals to your brain to trigger confident feelings.

The Sleeper

You can even practice power posing while you sleep. Amy Cuddy suggests lying on your back with your arms and legs outstretched, rather than curled up in the fetal position. You will wake up feeling bigger and more powerful.

When you can't practice these poses, simply remember in general to stand tall, open up, use eye contact, shoulders back, head held high, and smile. Remember to avoid looking down, slumping your shoulders, drawing in, crossing your arms and legs, and remaining expressionless. Just those few changes will go a long way in improving your feelings of confidence.

Changing your body language takes awareness and practice. But research has proven that the changes are well worth the investment in time and energy. Your body language tells a story about you the minute you walk in the room. Be sure the protagonist of your story is seen as the confident hero—even if it's a fairy tale for a while. Eventually the tale will be true.

Action Steps

What kind of body language do you generally use? How are you using low power poses or expressing yourself weakly through your body language?

Practice some or all of the power poses outlined in this chapter for two minutes every day. Look at yourself in the mirror as you practice, even if it feels silly.

Then choose a pose you feel you can try in a real world setting at work or in another environment (a party or family gathering). Pay attention to how you feel as you are posing and the reactions of those around you.

Chapter 12:
The Dynamic Duo of
Judgment and Intuition

THERE WAS A popular news story in 2007 about a cat that lived in a nursing home and consistently jumped on a patient's bed within a couple of hours of the person's death. Dogs often alert their owners before a health crisis occurs, like a heart attack or stroke. After the 2004 Indian Ocean tsunami, people reported seeing animals fleeing to higher ground minutes before the tsunami arrived. It appears animals have some kind of heightened intuitive sense to subtle changes in the environment and to the people around them. They are tuned in to changes in smell and vibratory shifts. It's clear that some animals can sense human emotion and respond to it. So do people have this same intuitive sense? It seems we do.

Scientific studies reveal that an area of the human brain called the anterior cingulate cortex actually raises the alarm about danger without ever penetrating the conscious mind. Human pheromones serve as chemical messengers that allow us to subtly communicate with others through our sense of smell. And we've all experienced the power of intuition in making decisions and choices in our lives. When logic, judgment, and intuition are combined, you have a powerful force for confidence. In fact, intuition seems to involve tapping in to our logic and judgment—very quickly.

Research published in *The British Journal of Psychology* suggests that intuitive experiences are based on the instantaneous evaluation of internal and external cues. Researchers concluded that intuition involves the brain quickly drawing on past experiences and external cues to make a decision on a non-conscious level. But it occurs so fast we're not aware the intuition actually stemmed from a burst of logical thinking.

This quote on psychodynamics (the study of cognitive, subconscious and primal neurological responses to sensory input and experiences) resonates with me as an explanation for our intuition:

> We tend to experience the higher levels of our intuition when dozens of conscious insights, subconscious memories and senses converge to bring forward a conclusive insight that would normally be beyond the scope of conscious calculation or cognitive explanation.

All we have learned, observed, and sensed comes together in a nanosecond the moment we need the information. Everything that makes us who we are can serve us on a very sophisticated and complex level that appears almost extrasensory. In the long run, I don't know if the "why" of our intuition is really so important. Whether these abilities can be explained by science or not, there's plenty of evidence they exist for all of us to some degree. If you agree with this premise, then I suggest what matters most is how we use these abilities to positively impact our self-confidence.

Unlike animals, most humans have an underdeveloped intuition because we don't pay much attention to it. We are so distracted by everything around us that we miss the subtleties of our subconscious or ignore the messages wafting around with our pheromones. We have been trained by a modern, technological society to look outward for answers rather than paying attention to the more refined sources of information inside ourselves. Our intuition has atrophied as a result. If we did pay attention to these sources on a regular basis, I think our lives would be strikingly different. Our world would be different. Our choices and decisions would be more thoroughly informed and grounded. We would sense and understand possible outcomes and deeper meanings. Our relationships and interactions with others would shift as we are more aware of the nuances of moods and demeanor. And we would feel more confident about our rational choices, especially when they are reinforced by intuitive urgings. If we combined intuition with logic and with our other five senses, we could harness the full power of our natural abilities in so many aspects of our lives.

Looking back at the 2004 tsunami, it wasn't just animals that fled before the big waves struck. The native tribes of Sri Lanka also fled to higher ground before the tsunami. Having had nearly 60,000 years of contact with the natural environment, these indigenous people emulated the animals, and they nearly all survived. These are people who do not depend on technology and must rely on their instincts and subtle cues from the environment for their very survival. When you trust and act on your intuition, you increase your confidence because you are building trust in yourself and your abilities. The combination of logic, judgment, and intuition is a powerful force for making successful decisions and choices. It affords a profound sense of security that no relationship, job, or amount of money will ever give you.

There are many ways to tune into your intuition and apply it's guidance and wisdom in your life. Here are a few:

Take Time to Pay Attention

If you don't slow down, you won't be able to focus on your intuition and the subtle messages sent to you by others. Don't cram your life with so much input that you are too busy to stop and acknowledge what your intuition is telling you.

Don't Ignore the Vibes You Receive

Have you ever met someone and felt immediately uncomfortable? Have you sensed that someone was staring at you? Have you had a sense of danger before anything bad has happened? Even if you feel foolish or gullible, don't ignore these signals. Take appropriate action, especially if you sense danger. You are receiving messages from your subconscious or being alerted by some very subtle physical changes or sensations.

Go Within and Ask a Question

If you are seeking a solution to a problem, trying to make a decision, or if you need a creative idea, go to a quiet place where you cannot be interrupted. Breathe deeply for several minutes and calm your thoughts. Then ask a question of your subconscious mind. Sit quietly and wait for 10 or 15 minutes. If you don't get an answer immediately, keep asking the question—before you go to bed, when you wake up, while you are in the car. The power and patterns of all of your senses, insights, logic, and memories will converge to provide guidance for you.

Write Down Your Dreams and Interpret Them

Your dreams are powerful subconscious dramas playing out while you sleep. They offer insight into your daily problems and life events through archetypal imagery and symbols. Do some research and reading on dream interpretation so that you can reap the full benefit of all of the messages and psychic support your dreams provide. Keep a dream journal and write down your dreams as soon as you remember them.

Keep a Journal for Stream of Consciousness Ideas

Writing is a very powerful way to tap into your subconscious and to strengthen your intuition. Keep a journal in which you write down thoughts that come to you without your specific focus or intention. I often start writing by first asking, "What do I need to know today?" You'd be amazed at what comes out on your paper. Don't analyze it while you're writing. Just write even if it seems non-nonsensical. Close the journal and then wait a day before you read it. As with dreams, this information might make more sense to you if you sit on it a while.

Visualize and Speak Your Intentions

Your subconscious mind, intuition and dreams regularly send messages to you. Try sending messages right back. Visualize what you want to accomplish or your end goal. Speak your intentions out loud as though they are already real. Reinforce your desires with your subconscious mind so that it can work for you to actualize what you want. I'm not suggesting some magical attraction. If you plant a subconscious seed, your mind and senses are going to help the seed germinate and bloom.

Listen to Others with All of Your Senses

Be fully engaged when you are listening to someone. Pay attention not only to the words, but also to expressions, smells, gestures and moods. Read the full person, not just the content of the language. In interpersonal relationships and business interactions, this is a dynamic and useful ability that can give you an edge and make you feel more confident. Some of these non-verbal cues are easy to pick up, but others are subtle and require "sensing" a person's real message. Pay full attention.

Spend Time in Nature Regularly

When you spend time in nature, you are stimulating and rekindling some of the ancient parts of your brain that were necessary for survival. You are tuning back to the natural order and creating a heightened sensitivity to the interrelatedness of all living things. You are refilling your "intuitive tank" so you have a surplus when you reenter the modern world.

Acknowledging and honing your intuitive abilities provides another layer of information and reinforcement as you work on your confidence. In areas where you might be lacking confidence, remember to tune into your intuition to bring stored information, ideas, and insights to the surface. Combine your intuition with logic and intelligence as you make important decisions. What should you do if intuition and logic are at odds? This scenario can undercut your self-confidence, but it doesn't have to. This is the time to seek reinforcements, phone a friend, talk to a mentor or counselor, and get a second or third opinion.

Examine whether it's your lack of confidence causing the confusion or a real disparity between intuition and judgment. If it's a true disparity, seek feedback, do your research, examine your true desires, and then simply make a choice based on the information at hand. Confidence means you are willing to take an occasional leap of faith after using all the tools at your disposal.

Action Steps

In what areas of your life can you slow down, pay more attention, and listen more carefully, so you can acknowledge what your intuition is telling you?

Are you currently seeking the answer to a problem, trying to make a decision, or looking for a creative solution? What questions can you ask your subconscious mind in order to gain clarity? Write the questions down, and then ask them to yourself. Sit quietly for 5-10 minutes and listen for an answer. What came up for you?

Chapter 13:
Raising Your EQ for
Confident Relationships

WHEN I AM coaching a client, often one of the most profound leaps they make is recognizing the personal power that accompanies adult decisions, outlooks, and behaviors. Sometimes a person is so entrenched in reactive behaviors, old hurts, and learned perceptions they don't realize they are trapped in a stage of childhood that limits their personal growth and hinders their relationships.

Much has been written in popular psychology about the concept of embracing one's inner child. In this context, I'm referring to the therapeutic work (usually offered by mental health professionals) to help clients heal the emotional wounds and coping mechanisms that arise from adverse childhood experiences. This inner child work includes helping people face and heal unresolved grief and unmet needs from childhood. Often this grief takes the form of depression, controlling behaviors, anger, intimacy problems, and poor communication skills. Facing and healing these hurts is critical to becoming a fully-functioning, healthy adult. Another big step toward becoming whole and healthy is embracing your inner adult. Sometimes we don't evolve into the grown-ups we are supposed to be because we've missed a stage in emotional development, or we simply didn't have appropriate role models or support systems. We don't understand or adopt appropriate adult behaviors and reactions.

Consistent relationship difficulties are often a clue that one's inner adult is begging to be released. These relationship difficulties can include intimate relationships, as well as relationships with friends, co-workers, and family members. If a running theme of complaints has developed over the years about your behaviors, reactions, or decisions with people close to you, then you need to look at yourself realistically and begin to make some changes.

In fact everyone needs to take the pulse of their inner adult now and then to make sure he or she is alive and well. A good way to take this pulse is to understand your Emotional Intelligence Quotient or EQ. Emotional intelligence, as defined by Wikipedia, "is the ability to monitor one's own and other people's emotions, to discriminate between different emotions and label them appropriately, and to use emotional information to guide thinking and behavior." The concept has been around for a while, but was made popular in Daniel Goleman's bestselling book, *Emotional Intelligence: Why it can matter more than IQ.* A person with a strong EQ regularly works on developing attitudes and behaviors in relation to himself and his environment which lift him past childishness and dependency. A person with a strong EQ is authentic, open, and willing to grow, learn, and accept her own flaws and mistakes.

Emotional intelligence is the ability to recognize your emotions, understand what they're telling you, and realize how your emotions affect people around you. When you seek to understand how others feel, this allows you to manage relationships more effectively and empathetically. According to Daniel Goleman's book: there are five major components of emotional intelligence skills:

Self-Awareness

People with high emotional intelligence are very self-aware. They've examined and understand their emotions, and don't let their feelings rule them. They understand the impact of their emotions on other people. They're also willing to take an honest look at themselves. They know their strengths and weaknesses and work on these areas so they can perform better. Many people believe that self-awareness is the most important part of emotional intelligence.

Self-Regulation

This is the ability to control emotions and impulses. People who self-regulate typically don't allow themselves to become too angry or jealous, and they don't make impulsive, careless decisions. They think before they act. Characteristics of self-regulation are thoughtfulness, comfort with change, integrity, and the ability to say no.

Motivation

People with a high degree of emotional intelligence are usually motivated. They're willing to defer immediate results for long-term success. They're highly productive, love a challenge, and are very effective in whatever they do.

Empathy

This is perhaps the second-most important element of emotional intelligence. Empathy is the ability to identify with and understand the wants, needs, and viewpoints of those around you. People with empathy are good at recognizing the feelings of others, even when those feelings may not be obvious. As a result, empathetic people are usually excellent at managing relationships, listening, and relating to others. They avoid stereotyping and judging too quickly, and they live their lives in a very open, honest way.

Social Skills

It's usually easy to talk to and like people with good social skills, another sign of high emotional intelligence. Those with strong social skills are typically team players. Rather than focus on their own success first, they help others develop and shine. They can manage disputes, are excellent communicators, and are masters at building and maintaining relationships.

The good news is that emotional intelligence CAN be taught and developed. Many books and tests are available to help you determine your current EQ and identify where you may need to do some work. You can also use these tips:

1. Observe how you react to people. Do you rush to judgment before you know all of the facts? Do you stereotype? Look honestly at how you think and interact with other people. Try to put yourself in their place, and be more open and accepting of their perspectives and needs.

2. Look at your work environment. Do you seek attention for your accomplishments? Humility can be a wonderful quality, and it doesn't mean that you're shy or lack self-confidence. When you practice humility, you can be quietly confident about your successes. Give others a chance to shine—put the focus on them, and don't worry too much about getting praise for yourself.

3. Do a self-evaluation. What are your weaknesses? Are you willing to accept that you're not perfect and that you could work on some areas to make yourself a better person? Have the courage to look at yourself honestly and make changes as a result of what you see.

4. Examine how you react to stressful situations. Do you become upset every time there's a delay or something doesn't happen the way you want? Do you blame others or become angry at them, even when it's not their fault? The ability to stay calm and in control in difficult situations is highly

valued—in the business world and outside it. Keep your emotions under control when things go wrong.

5. Take responsibility for your actions. Have you recently hurt someone's feelings or offended someone? If so, apologize directly—don't ignore what you did or avoid the person. People are usually more willing to forgive and forget if you make an honest attempt to make things right.

6. Examine how your actions will affect others— before you take those actions. If your decision will impact others, put yourself in their place. How will they feel if you do this? Would you want that experience? If you must take the action, how can you help others deal with the effects?

As you develop your emotional intelligence, you will see how your self-confidence improves. You will naturally attract other people to you, and you will feel more empowered and in control of your reactions and emotions. The skills may not be natural at first, but continue to notice how you might be acting in ways that don't reflect a high EQ. Awareness is the first step toward change.

Action Steps

Review the six tips in this chapter, and answer the questions in writing listed in each tip. Consider specific actions you can take to improve your emotional intelligence.

If you would like to find out more about your emotional intelligence quotient, you can take a free emotional intelligence test online. There are a variety of free tests available if you Google "free emotional intelligence test."

Chapter 14:
The Financial Cost of
Low Confidence

THERE IS LITTLE doubt that low self-confidence can hinder your financial success. In fact, believing in yourself and your ability to be successful may be more important than other seemingly more influential factors such as family wealth, education and demographics. If you were born into a well-educated, affluent family, you do have a financial advantage. But when you add the element of self-confidence in the mix, your ability to become financially successful increases dramatically.

"There are certainly significant advantages for children growing up with parents who are well-educated and work in professional occupations, but these advantages are especially profound when children are self-confident," says Dr. Timothy Judge in the *Journal of Applied Psychology*. However, lacking the silver spoon factor doesn't destine you to low confidence or prevent you from being financially successful. Confidence is such a decisive factor that people who come from blue-collar families and have confidence earn approximately $7,000 more a year than those from the same social class who lack confidence. Likewise, people from the professional classes who have confidence earn approximately $28,000 more than people without confidence.

"In light of popular beliefs that kids from middle- and upper-class families have it made, it is surprising to see what little positive impact socioeconomic status has in the absence of self-esteem," says Dr. Judge. Research reveals that people with a positive attitude who believe in themselves and their ability to succeed have more ambitious goals, leading to higher incomes. Even when they encounter adversity, they're not as likely to internalize it or allow it to impact their success.

However, people with low self-confidence often engage in subconscious behaviors that undermine their success, making them less likely to ask for or get promotions, raises and even jobs. And unfortunately, bosses, clients, and customers make assumptions about people who exhibit behaviors of low confidence. Those with low confidence are less likely to speak up in meetings or to take on challenging tasks, which can lead superiors to believe they are ineffective, lazy, or lacking intelligence.

The bottom line is this: having self-confidence pays. Whether you're a lawyer or a brick-layer, if you have confidence, you're much more likely to make a better income than those with low confidence. Knowing this fact might initially make you feel worse about your financial future, but remember—you are reading this book to work on your confidence. For every incremental amount you improve your self-confidence, you're overcoming obstacles to your financial success. You're empowering yourself to feel good about your abilities, to take risks, to ask for the job or the raise, to speak up in meetings.

Just one confident action could win you the account, give you a salary jump, or snare that small business loan. An accumulation of these actions will make a profound impact on your financial future. Of course self-confidence further affords the motivation to manage your money effectively, to make wise financial decisions, to go after additional training or education, and to set realistic yet challenging financial goals. There are some practical techniques for dealing with confidence barriers to your financial success which you can implement on a daily basis before work, before you ask for a raise or try to close a deal, or simply when you are feeling low confidence.

Exercise

The effects of exercise on your confidence are so overwhelming it can't be understated. During exercise, your body releases endorphins that give you a boost of energy and positive feelings. Simply the accomplishment of completing an exercise routine will give you a boost of confidence you can carry with you throughout the day.

Appearance

I've mentioned this in previous chapters and want to reemphasize the dramatic effect your appearance and your feelings about your appearance can have on your confidence level. Especially if you work around other people, take the steps to assess and improve your appearance in realistic ways. Update your wardrobe, take care of your teeth and hair, and maintain a healthy weight. Whether or not we like it, others judge us and our abilities by our appearance. When your appearance is in sync with how you want people to view you, confidence will follow.

Body Language

Remember, people with powerful body language feel more confident. Even if you fake the power poses mentioned previously, they will trick your brain into having confident feelings. Timid body language tends to limit feelings of confidence.

Practice

Whenever you see the opportunity to increase your financial success, take action. You won't get the raise unless you ask for it. You won't snag the better position unless you negotiate. The worst that could happen is getting a "no." A "no" doesn't mean you aren't worth it, you aren't good enough, or they don't like you. A "no" is an invitation to try again more creatively, or it's reflection of a legitimate reason for "not this time."

Define

Define what financial success means to you. You may have a salary number in mind, or it may be a lifestyle you desire that requires a certain level of income. Define what that is and write it down. Then think of everything you need to do to reach that salary or income level. Consider every possible practical action required to move you closer to that level in the next year. Keep that income posted where you can see it every day to motivate you toward action.

As you continue to work on your confidence, it's likely you will see a direct correlation between your increased confidence and your level of income. Let that knowledge inspire and motivate you to continue to take small manageable actions to push past your comfort zone and challenge yourself for greater financial success.

Action Steps

How do you think your work superiors, peers, and clients view your level of self-confidence? Can you think of specific ways your lack of confidence has impacted your financial success?

What specific actions are you willing to take to improve your confidence on the job; to get additional training or education you might need for your work; to change limiting work circumstances you can't control; and to become adept at managing money?

Chapter 15:
Practice and Present
Moment Awareness

WHEN I WAS a child, I took both piano lessons and violin lessons. The idea of being a proficient pianist or violinist was very appealing. I remember getting my violin and showing it to all of my friends. It sat in a green velvet-lined case, gleaming and smelling of rosin, like a beautiful, untouchable artifact in a museum. My friends look at it with awe, and I felt proud—even though I hadn't had my first lesson. I didn't comprehend when I began my lessons with both instruments that simply owning a piano or violin didn't guarantee my proficiency or confidence as a musician. I understood I had to take lessons. I didn't understand how much practice was involved.

Practice felt like work, like the drudgery you had to endure in order to arrive at Carnegie Hall one day. As Malcolm Gladwell reminds in the book *Outliers: The Story of Success*, it takes 10,000 hours of practice to become a world-class expert at something. It certainly takes thousands of hours over time simply to become proficient. Practice is not only an essential ingredient in proficiency. It is the bricks and mortar of self-confidence.

> If you want to write, you practice writing.
> If you want to be an artist, you practice your art.

> If you want to be a lawyer, you practice law.
> If you want to serve, you practice serving.

> If you want to feel confident about any ability, practice, effort, and experience are essential. You must be willing to endure both the discomfort of being a beginner at something, as well as the discipline required of practice. More importantly, you must learn to lean in to practice.

Martha Graham, the foremost pioneer of modern dance, speaks eloquently of the power of practice in for a 1952 radio interview on *This I Believe*:

> I believe that we learn by practice. Whether it means to learn to dance by practicing dancing or to learn to live by practicing living, the principles are the same. In each, it is the performance of a dedicated precise set of acts, physical or intellectual, from which comes shape of achievement, a sense of one's being, a satisfaction of spirit. One becomes, in some area, an athlete of God. Practice means to perform, over and over again in the face of all obstacles, some act of vision, of faith, of desire. Practice is a means of inviting the perfection desired.

As you practice, even before you reach a stage of mastery, your self-confidence will improve. You will have solid evidence that practice affords skill. You will have evidence that you are capable of achievement. Yes, there is a certain amount of drudgery involved in practice. But if you are intently focused on it, practice can be deeply satisfying.

When I was taking piano and violin lessons, my sister Jesse was taking piano and cello lessons. We both took our lessons for a few years, and then we both quit after driving our mother crazy by constantly whining about practice. As a result, I never felt confident about my musical abilities. Jesse, however, has taken up cello again as an adult. She quit when she was twelve and started again at age fifty. She practices every day and finds great joy in it. Here is what she wrote to me about practice:

> I've come to understand that my real passion is practice and the experience of flow that comes as its result. By practice I mean any discipline which allows a person to cultivate themselves over a long period of time.

> I don't think school as I experienced it taught me how to learn. I don't remember having teachers whom I truly respected or ever feeling that I had waded into endless depths with immense joy.

> In my twenties I discovered the Japanese martial art of Aikido. Over twenty years of practice, in some years five times a week, I believe I have bowed to a partner or a teacher almost 100,000 times. These are

full bows, all the way to the floor simply to begin practice or to thank another for trusting their body to me. I love the unstinting generosity of spirit that practice demands. I love the repetition accompanied by the demand that one deepen, deepen, deepen.

There is a story about a man who approached a renowned martial arts teacher asking to study with him. The teacher asked him why he wanted to learn martial arts. "To defend myself." "Ah" the teacher said, "and which self do you want to defend?" I have loved coming to know the different selves which have evolved over the years of training.

Some years ago I found that the injuries I had accumulated over time prevented me from training. It would be difficult to describe the grief I felt. After a period of what felt like aimlessness, I begin endurance running. During that same period I had adopted a child. I came to see that the practice of Aikido, with its fixed schedule, would have been almost impossible given the real time demands of parenting. I was grateful for the solitude of running (and for the fact that I could run at 4:00 a.m. and be home before my son woke up). Again, after some years injuries ended my practice. Five years ago I began the practice of the cello.

The rituals of tuning, rosining my bow, wiping the dust off my cello replace the training uniform, the bows to a partner, the repeated falls. My teacher reminds me,

as my Aikido sensei did, as my running mentors did,
to relax my shoulder, to open my face, to practice in
the spirit of joy.

When you practice in the spirit of joy, you are not only
improving your confidence, but also you're giving yourself
the gift of present moment awareness. You are allowing
practice to shift from simply a means to an end to an
exercise in mindfulness and engagement. You don't have to
allow the dread of practice to serve as a reason to avoid it.
Begin to view practice as an opportunity for joy. Your
opportunities for improving your confidence in any area of
your life are only limited to your imagination and your
willingness to engage. Every day we are presented with
many different opportunities to improve our self-confidence
simply through the act of engaging in practice. If you fall
back on the excuse that you are not confident because you
aren't skilled at something, then by all means, become
skilled. You may tell yourself you don't have the ability, the
intellect, or the means to accomplish something—but the
vast majority of the time, these are simply stories that keep
us stuck.

One of my favorite scenes from Jane Austen's *Pride and
Prejudice* is the one in which Elizabeth Bennet, as she is
playing the piano rather poorly, sets Mr. Darcy straight when
he offers excuses for his poor social skills.

"I certainly have not the talent which some people
possess," said Darcy, "of conversing easily with those
I have never seen before. I cannot catch their tone of

conversation, or appear interested in their concerns, as I often see done.

"My fingers," said Elizabeth, "do not move over this instrument in the masterly manner which I see so many women's do. They have not the same force or rapidity, and do not produce the same expression. But then I have always supposed it to be my own fault— because I would not take the trouble of practicing. It is not that I do not believe my fingers as capable as any other woman's of superior execution" (Austen, p 132).

Ms. Bennet may not feel confident in her musical skills, but she does have the confidence and self-awareness to know she isn't lacking the ability, only the discipline. If you find yourself lacking confidence in a particular area of your life, perhaps it has less to do with your general abilities and more to do with an unwillingness to put in the time and effort necessary to become proficient. If your lack of self-confidence has undermined your motivation to expend time and effort, remember that motivation and confidence increase with every effort you make toward practice. You don't need motivation or confidence to begin. Start small. Invest just a little time every day, but remain consistent. As you feel your motivation and engagement increase, begin to add more practice time.

Whatever it is you want to achieve, just start doing that thing. Do it over and over until you get better and better. Before too long, you will see how practice leads to a joyful confidence not only in your achievement, but also in your day-to-day efforts toward mastery.

Action Steps

Are any of your confidence challenges related to a pursuit or activity in which you lack proficiency or skill? Are you willing to take the time to become more skilled and proficient? What kind of commitment are you willing to make to yourself in order to practice or work on one or more of these pursuits?

Chapter 16:
Confident Decision Making and Problem Solving

AS YOU WORK on rebuilding your confidence, there's no better place to hone your skills than learning to make decisions and solving the inevitable problems life throws your way. When you lack confidence, you feel paralyzed. You don't trust yourself or believe you have what it takes to make the right choices or to handle difficulties properly. Every decision or problem is excruciating because you aren't assured you have the judgment, knowledge, or discernment to take action. So you simply do nothing and allow events to play out on their own—often with disappointing or even harmful consequences.

It's critically important to your confidence work that you learn to act *in spite* of your fears and doubts, rather than remaining stuck in inertia. As Teddy Roosevelt once said, "In any moment of decision, the best thing you can do is the right thing, the next best thing is the wrong thing, and the worst thing you can do is nothing." Why is doing nothing the worst thing you can do? Because inaction not only allows problems and decisions to remain unaddressed, but also it further deflates your confidence and makes you feel powerless. By practicing the skills of making decisions and solving problems in small and manageable situations, you can begin to feel comfortable with the process.

There are two parts to improving your confidence by working on decision making and problem solving. First, there are the emotional aspects—overcoming or managing the fearful and uncomfortable feelings that arise when you are faced with a decision or problem. Secondly, there's the logical and intellectual process you must follow when preparing to act on a decision or problem. Learning the latter will help you with the former. As you rely on your logic, judgment, and time-tested processes for evaluating problems and choices, you'll feel more secure that you're taking correct action with whatever situation arises in your life. With practice, you'll become increasingly adept at dealing with problems and decisions, and even when situations don't turn out as you might hope, you'll feel confident you did your best, and that you have the courage to take action in the future.

Here are some steps to take before you make any large or small decisions:

1. Define your values and personal operating system before you are faced with decisions.

This should be the foundation and reference point for every decision you make. In your deepest dreams, how do you envision your life in all areas—career, relationships, finances, lifestyle, etc. What core values does your vision reflect or support?

Be sure you write down your personal operating system and the values that define it, and refine these over time as necessary. Then when a big decision comes along, you can use these as a guide. Look at the various outcomes of each side of the decision. Does one outcome move you closer to your vision? If you deviate too far from your vision, you'll eventually experience pain and regret. Evaluate your choices based on your vision. Which one is in closest alignment with it?

2. Evaluate the pros and cons.

Consider the possible positive and negative outcomes of your decision. Write down a list of pros and cons for each possible alternative. Then prioritize these points with the most important considerations at the top of the list.

- What are the possible implications of the cons?

- Do they outweigh the pros?

- Can you live with the potential negative fallout or consequences?

- What could you do to mitigate the fallout?

If you have a big decision that involves many smaller decisions, follow this pros and cons process for each of these decisions.

3. Seek guidance and feedback.

Carefully select two or three trusted friends or advisers whose opinion and judgment you value. Tell them about your personal operating system, show them your list of pros and cons, and ask for their input about your decision. Someone who is distanced from the turmoil of the decision and has a different perspective can help you see things in a clearer light. A personal coach or counselor also can help you gain clarity around your decision by asking you pointed questions related to your motivations, feelings, and desires. The point here is not to rely totally on the advice of others, but to use it in the mix of the decision-making process.

4. Take time for reflection.

Allow yourself a few days to sit on the information you have gathered and the ideas that have come up. Visualize yourself in each possible outcome of the decision, thinking about the possible positive and negative implications of each. What feels like the best decision? What does your intuition tell you when you visualize all possible outcomes?

5. Set a reasonable and public deadline.

After you've gone through this decision making process, you must take action. Set a reasonable deadline for yourself and announce it publicly. Even if you aren't completely certain, make a decision. It is rare when you feel 100 percent sure about any decision, so expect ambiguous feelings. Once you have done the work, honored your vision, examined the pros and cons, and sought guidance, make your choice, take the leap and don't look back. There are millions of paths we can take in a lifetime, all leading to different opportunities and potential consequences. You won't have a guarantee, but you don't need one. Uncertainty is part of the adventure of life.

Problem Solving

Problem solving is very similar to decision making but is usually more complex. When you encounter a problem in life or work, often there are other people involved and many possible scenarios to consider. The most important first step in problem solving is temporarily stepping out of the emotions involved, whether it's fear, anger, disappointment, or frustration, and approaching the problem analytically. You can always revisit the emotions, but allow yourself a break from them so you have a clear head.

Here is a very simple five-step process when you are faced with a problem:

1. Define the problem.

This seems intuitive, but in the cloud of our emotions, we want to be sure we know what we're dealing with. Identify the problem as specifically as possible, evaluating the present situation and determining how it differs from the desired outcome or state.

2. Analyze the problem.

Analyzing involves learning as much as you can about the problem. It may be necessary to look beyond the obvious, surface situation to stretch your imagination and see a variety of possibilities and implications. You don't want a knee-jerk reaction before you really understand what you're dealing with.

3. Develop possible solutions.

Identify a wide range of possible solutions through brainstorming with others, thinking about ways you've dealt with similar problems, and even researching how others have dealt with this problem.

4. Evaluate each solution.

Weigh the pros and cons of each solution as outlined with decision making. Think through each solution and consider what is most realistic, provides the best outcome, and has the least negative consequences. Consider both immediate and long-term results.

5. Make a choice for a solution.

Based on what you have learned about the problem and possible solutions, take action right away. Address problems as quickly as possible so you don't have the energy drain of it hanging over your head.

Fear, doubt, and discomfort are inevitable when faced with problems and decisions—even for the most self-confident people. Uncertainty and life difficulties create angst for all of us. You can mitigate these feelings when you have a plan of action and a sound process. Confidence develops when you learn to follow a process in spite of your feelings and take decisive action once you complete the process. The more you do it, the easier it will become and the better you will feel about yourself and your abilities.

Action Steps

What are the decisions or problems you are facing right now? Write them down in order of most concerning to least concerning.

Begin taking action on each of these decisions and problems by following the steps outlined in this chapter. Once you complete the process for each decision or problem, set a date for taking action and mark it on your calendar. For accountability, tell someone you trust about your plans and your action date.

Barrie Davenport

Chapter 17:
The Power of Personal Responsibility

ULTIMATELY, YOUR SELF-CONFIDENCE is in your own hands. You may have a variety of reasons for having low confidence, many of which have been painful and chronic. You have many unpleasant feelings around low self-confidence, feelings that make you want to retreat and continue to avoid the things that make you feel incapable, unsure, or incompetent. Sometimes it seems so much easier just to accept low confidence and operate within the confines of what feels non-threatening and comfortable. It's easier to barricade ourselves with excuses, blame, guilt, and fear.

However, we are no longer children, and we can't continue to hide behind the barricade if we want to succeed in the adult world. We must take personal responsibility for our own happiness, which means addressing the causes for our confidence problems and practicing the skills we've learned to rebuild our confidence. Here's what one of my readers on my blog "Live Bold and Bloom" once wrote me in response to a post on my most life-altering beliefs:

> A big one that I would like to add is taking personal responsibility. For years I thought I understood this

but really didn't. I didn't want to admit it, but I did a lot of blaming. At a very low point in my life when I felt that nothing I did was working (I used to be a control freak too), I felt like I gave up. In hindsight, I realized that I didn't give up. I just decided to accept everything and everyone the way they were. I let my feelings be known and accepted whatever came next. Now I take full responsibility for my actions and my circumstances. When things aren't the way I would like them to be, I look at how I got myself into the situation and how I can get myself out. I apologize more. I feel more open and compassionate of others. Things are easier, and I'm a lot happier.

This reader's attitude reflects a huge leap in her emotional maturity and self-confidence. She no longer blames, goes belly-up, or accepts whatever life throws at her. She has empowered herself. The essence of self-empowerment is personal responsibility—taking full and complete control and accountability for your own life and circumstances. This is both liberating and scary.

It's liberating because taking full responsibility for your life means you . . .

- make your own choices and decisions;

- live according to your own personal operating system and values;

- are free from the anxiety of living up to the expectations of others;

- experience the joy of being authentically yourself.

But it's frightening because you . . .

- can no longer blame others for your failures and disappointments;

- know you must step up to your potential;

- can't cling to childish, dependent security from others;

- have to let go of the "old you," even if that person was holding you back.

However, as you empower yourself through personal responsibility, those fears begin to dissipate. You find your confidence soars, things are easier, and life is more enjoyable because you are creating it on your own terms rather than reacting to your fears or outside circumstances. Relinquishing responsibility for your self-confidence issues means you are giving away your power through fear and blaming. You are allowing the winds of fate to rule you and resigning yourself to a compromised life. The more you do this, the more your self-esteem suffers. It's hard to respect yourself when you allow your lack of confidence to hold you back from your potential.

So how can you step up to your personal responsibility and empower yourself with confidence? First, examine yourself and take a hard look at your life to see where you might be giving away your power.

- How are you letting other people define or control you or your behavior?

- Who are you blaming for your confidence problems?

- What are you avoiding, and what excuses are you giving yourself and others?

Next, kill the victim mentality. Self-empowered people don't see themselves as victims. They view themselves as creators, catalysts, and thrivers. You may not even recognize you embrace a victim mentality. It could be deeply entrenched in your psyche from being victimized in the past. Sometimes it even feels good to be a victim because it brings sympathy and attention—but that's all you get from it. Sympathy and attention aren't enough for a confident, happy life.

Part of being a victim involves perpetuating a "story" about yourself that you repeat to explain why you are lacking confidence and why you behave the way you do. All of us have these stories, and they are based in some truth. You had a bad childhood. You lost your job. Your spouse left you. Your business failed. Everyone has suffered, and some have had truly debilitating life events. However, if you use these situations as the constant backdrop for your life, you will never escape being the leading character of a sad drama. The more you reinforce your story, the more entrenched you become in it.

Embracing personal responsibility for your life doesn't happen overnight. You have to practice. You need to do the things self-empowered people do until you gain mastery and confidence. Begin by actively shifting your thoughts away from victim language and toward success language. Try to catch yourself in thoughts of blame, shame, guilt, or self-pity. Then replace those thoughts with words of confidence, gratitude, self-love, and acceptance. Support your new thinking with real action. Where you once said, "I can't, I'm too weak, I'm too afraid," take one small action in the direction of "you can." Every small action will empower you.

Contrary to popular belief, taking personal responsibility for your confidence often means embracing support from other people. Asking for help does not mean you are weak or incapable. It means you are empowered enough to take full responsibility for your own personal evolution by seeking another way to expedite your awareness, confidence, and knowledge. This help can come in the form of books, courses, therapy, coaching, and the counsel of friends and family. Everyone, even the most self-confident, can benefit from the support and insights of others who have our best interest at heart.

Remember, you are responsible for building your confidence—you are the CEO of your own happiness. You CAN change the way you feel about yourself and your abilities through practice of the techniques outlined in this book. However, no one else can make you practice or push past the feelings of doubt and discomfort to take action on the things YOU want to accomplish. Every day reclaim your personal power by accepting full and total responsibility for your confidence and actions. Over time, you will see how profoundly your efforts have paid off, as you feel more and more sure of yourself, your abilities, and your capacity for a happy, successful life.

Action Steps

How are you letting other people define or control you or your behavior? Who are you blaming for any confidence issues or other problems in your life?

How might you be perpetuating a victim mentality? What is the "story" you tell to keep it going?

What are you willing to do to take personal responsibility for who you are, your choices and behaviors, and your life right now?

Write down your thoughts and answers to these questions.

Chapter 18:
Creating a Lifetime of Confidence

WHEN YOU BEGAN reading this book, your confidence wasn't where you wanted it to be. Yet you did have *enough* confidence to begin reading and taking actions to improve. So please take a moment to feel proud and grateful you took the initiative. You made a proactive decision to take control of your life by working hard to build your confidence, and now you've nearly completed the building blocks to confidence outlined in this book. I hope today, after completing this book, you're feeling a big improvement in your confidence level.

If you've been practicing the action steps and ideas outlined in this book, take a moment to reflect on how much your confidence improved over the last few weeks. Just a few shifts and behavior changes can trigger seismic improvements in your life. But your goal isn't to stop here— it's to have a lifetime of self-confidence. Your goal is to see yourself differently, to have new ways of thinking and behaving, and to love and embrace yourself for the unique, amazing person you are all the time—or at least most of the time.

If you've spent years struggling with low self-confidence, then it will take time and daily practice until confidence feels natural for you. As I've mentioned several times, you have to retrain your brain to really believe what you're teaching it. If you remember nothing else from this book, please remember that confidence CAN be learned, just like any other skill. However, unlike most other skills, becoming proficient at self-confidence will improve every other part of your life. When you believe in yourself, like yourself, and have a healthy, accepting attitude about your flaws and past failures, everything in your life improves tenfold. Your energy is no longer drained by worrying about how you appear to others or how bad you feel about yourself. Isn't that what you want from now on, for the rest of your life?

So how do you achieve a lifetime of self-confidence? In the closing chapter, I'll discuss some specific next steps you can take. Before we get to those, I want to be sure you understand one thing that will be required of you as you move past this book. You need to make a solid commitment to yourself to work on your confidence every single day. It needs to become a habit, like brushing your teeth or putting on your shoes. Without this commitment, you won't do the work, plain and simple. Without the work, you'll go back to your confidence set-point—the place you started when you began this book.

I've presented plenty of tools, ideas, and actions to work with. You have access to these tools forever, but you can't close the book and just walk away. I am asking you to commit to ten to fifteen minutes a day, preferably first thing in the morning, during which you do something to solidify and reinforce your confidence. This could include going over the previous chapters and action steps, speaking affirmations out loud, writing a gratitude list, or some combination of these. Begin your day with a confidence booster shot. Make your self-confidence work a top daily priority until it feels completely natural for you, which could take several more months. Even after that, go back to the work every time you feel your confidence slipping. There's no magic bullet here. Confidence takes practice. So please—commit to the practice.

Action Steps

Where do you still need to work on your confidence? What daily actions will you take to reinforce your confidence based on the ideas you've learned in this book? Go back and review the chapters if you need ideas.

Write down specific actions you will take every day, how long you will spend on the actions, and the time of day you will work on them. Put them on your calendar, or create a reminder on your phone or computer.

Create a commitment to yourself in writing that you'll follow through on these actions. Sign the commitment, show it to your family and friends, and post it where you can see it daily.

Conclusion and Next Steps

SO HERE YOU are, at the end of Building Confidence. Simply by reading this book, you've revealed a deep longing to become the person you want to be, the person you were meant to be. I hope you acknowledge the amazing step you have taken. Very few people take control of their lives this way and take personal responsibility for making real change. Low confidence isn't your fate or your life sentence. You not only have every right to embrace self-confidence, but you must embrace it to claim the full enjoyment of your experience on this Earth. Now you have the tools to work with and the knowledge to empower you. Now you see yourself more clearly—what's been holding you back and how to move forward.

Days or weeks after you finish this book, it will be easy to slip back into old routines and old ways of thinking. Your automatic responses to life's difficulties or fearful situations will try to creep back in. You've spent years building these responses but just a short time trying to undo them. You'll need to maintain your commitment to practicing the new skills you have learned and the new ways of thinking you've adopted. Continue with small confidence-building goals until your confidence is at a level to tackle more challenging goals. Over time, the self-confidence mindset will be your new fallback position. You will see that life ebbs and flows, with good times and disappointments, but your confidence remains steady.

I would like to leave you with a few reminders and next steps as you continue on your journey toward self-confidence.

- Remember, rarely are your beliefs about yourself the truth, the whole truth, or nothing but the truth. Challenge your negative beliefs with evidence to the contrary and substitute old beliefs with new, positive thoughts.

- Recognize that you are not alone. Everyone has suffered or still suffers from self-confidence issues. Self-confident people are those who have taken enough actions *in spite* of fear so that fear no longer has a hold on them.

- Play to your strengths. Acknowledge them and be grateful for them. Work on your weaknesses, but view them as small children who need your love and understanding, not shaming. Everyone has areas of strength and weakness. Some people just tend to focus on one or the other.

- Acknowledge the role that past events or wounds have played in your current life experience, but don't dwell there. Do the work required to heal from trauma, but keep focused on the reality of right now, as well as the goals you want to achieve.

- If depression or anxiety prevent you from taking action, make getting better your first priority. Go to the doctor and/or a counselor. Don't put this off. You can't grow into a self-confident person if you are constantly feeling depressed.

- If you suffer from "approval addiction," go back over Chapter 7 on people pleasing, and keep working to detach from the need to please. When you approve of yourself, others (who matter) will be naturally drawn to you.

- Keep your personal operating system and core values in a place where you can see them regularly. If you stay true to these in your decisions and actions, you can't go wrong. Make practical use of these every day.

- Exercise always makes you feel better about yourself. So does eating healthy, socializing, spending time in nature, connecting with your spirituality, and being creative. When you are feeling bad, do one of these things.

- Stay out of your head as much as possible. If you are prone to negative thinking, practice the "rubber band trick" and re-frame your thoughts. Then go do something. Action is creative and moves you forward.

- If you want to feel confident about a skill—practice, practice, practice. Nothing helps confidence like mastery and accomplishment.

- Revisit the strategies in this book every day, until it self-confidence feels natural for you. Keep notes or a journal about your goals, actions, and accomplishments toward confidence. Remind yourself of what you have accomplished and what you want to work on. Keep this book as a lifetime tool to help you stay on the self-confidence track.

Finally, remind yourself of how many days you have left if you live to age ninety. Go on, add them up. It is a finite number, and one day you will reach the last number. How many of those precious days do you want to give away to self-doubt, anxiety, and fear? How long will you hold yourself back? Every day, mentally place your fears and doubts in a box and put them up on a shelf. Then create each and every day exactly the way you want it—without the presence of fear and doubt. One day you'll revisit this box and discover it's empty. Your doubts and fears have disappeared because you were too busy living a confident life.

Thank you so much for joining me on this confidence-building journey. You have something vital and beautiful to offer the world, your community, your friends and family. It was my pleasure to support you on this path and help you embrace the amazing, confident person you are.

Did You Like *Building Confidence*?

THANK YOU SO much for purchasing *Building Confidence.* I'm honored by the trust you've placed in me and my work by choosing this book to improve your confidence. I truly hope you've enjoyed it and found it useful for your life.

I'd like to ask you for a small favor. Could you please take just a minute to leave a review for this book on Amazon? This feedback will help me continue to write the kind of Kindle books that will best serve you. If you really loved the book, please let me know!

Another Book You Might Enjoy from Barrie Davenport

The 52-Week Life Passion Project:
The Path to Uncover Your Life Passion

There is also an accompanying *Project Workbook*,
filled with actions and lessons.

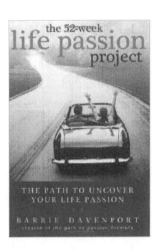 

These books are available through Amazon.com in
Kindle and paperback versions.

Want to Learn More?

IF YOU'D LIKE to learn more about confidence and self-esteem, please visit my blog Live Bold and Bloom (www.liveboldandbloom.com) for more articles, or check out my online course, Simple Self-Confidence (http://simpleselfconfidence.com).

Notes

Chapter 2: What Does DNA Have to Do with It?

Behavioral geneticist Corina Greven of King's College in London (Corina U. Greven, Nicole Harlaar, Yulia Kovas, Tomas Chamorro-Premuzic, and Robert Plomin. "More Than Just IQ: School Achievement Is Predicted by Self-Perceived Abilities—But for Genetic Rather Than Environmental Reasons," 2009, vol. 20, no. 6, 753-762.)

According to Healy, there are a host of behaviors and mindsets— from exercise to self-awareness (Healy, Maureen D. "Is Self-Confidence Pre-Determined." Psychology Today.com. Web. 3 Nov. 2011.)

For those of us introverts who live in Western Cultures ("Extraversion and introversion." Wikipedia.org. n.d. Web.)

Chapter 6: Mirror Mirror—How Appearance Can Shatter Self-Assurance

According to a study from the Center of Appearance Research (Campbell, Denis. "Body image concerns more men than women, research finds." The Guardian.com. Web. 5 Jan. 2012.)

Chapter 7: People Pleasing and Perfectionism

According to transformational psychologist (Earley, Jay. "The People-Pleasing Pattern." Personal Growth Programs.com. Web. n.d.)

Chapter 11: Your Body Speaks Volumes

Social psychologist Amy Cuddy (Cuddy, Amy. "Your body language shapes who you are." Online video clip. Ted.com. June 2012.)

Alexander Todorov, a psychologist and professor (Boutin, Chad. "To determine election outcomes, study says snap judgments are sufficient." Princeton.edu. Web. 22 Oct. 2007.)

Chapter 12: The Dynamic Duo of Judgment and Intuition

Research published in *The British Journal of Psychology* (Hodgkinson, G.P., Langan-Fox, J. and Sadler-Smith, E. (2008). "Intuition: A fundamental bridging construct in the behavioural sciences." British Journal of Psychology, 99, 1-27.)

This quote on psychodynamics, (Finkleman, Harold. "A note on the Science of Intuition." Web. members.shaw.ca. n.d.)

Chapter 14: The Financial Cost of Low Confidence

"There are certainly significant advantages for children (Judge, T. A., Hurst, C., & Simon, L. S. (2009). "Does it pay to be smart, attractive, or confident (or all three)?: Relationships among general mental ability, physical attractiveness, core self-evaluations, and income," Journal of Applied Psychology, 94, 742-755.)

Printed in Great Britain
by Amazon.co.uk, Ltd.,
Marston Gate.